60* Quick Cowls

60 Quick Cowls

LUXURIOUS PROJECTS
TO KNIT IN **CLOUD**™
AND **DUO**™ YARNS
FROM **CASCADE YARNS**®

THE EDITORS OF
SIXTH&SPRING BOOKS

sixth&springbooks NEW YORK

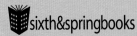

sixth&springbooks

161 Avenue of the Americas, NEW YORK, NY 10013
sixthandspringbooks.com

Managing Editor
LAURA COOKE

Senior Editor
LISA SILVERMAN

Yarn Editor
VANESSA PUTT

Editorial Assistant
SARAH THIENEMAN

Supervising Patterns
Editor
CARLA SCOTT

Patterns Editors
RENEE LORION
LORI STEINBERG

Photography
JACK DEUTSCH

Stylists
JOANNA RADOW
KATHERINE VILLALON

Hair and Makeup
ELENA LYAKIR

Vice President
TRISHA MALCOLM

Publisher
CAROLINE KILMER

Creative Director
JOE VIOR

Production Manager
DAVID JOINNIDES

President
ART JOINNIDES

Chairman
JAY STEIN

Library of Congress Cataloging-in-Publication Data

60 quick cowls : luxurious projects to knit in cloud and duo yarns from cascade yarns / by The editors of Sixth&Spring Books. — First edition.
pages cm
ISBN 978-1-936096-93-0
1. Cowls (Clothing) 2. Knitting—Patterns. I. Sixth & Spring Books. II. Title: Sixty quick cowls.
TT825.A12484 2015
746.43'20432—dc23
2015007377

Manufactured in China

1 3 5 7 9 10 8 6 4 2

First Edition

CASCADE YARNS
DISTRIBUTOR OF FINE YARN

cascadeyarns.com

contents

1 Riches of Ribs 18
2 Leaning Tower 20
3 Cable & Bobble Combo 22
4 Gorgeous Gathers 25
5 Fetching Feather & Fan 28
6 Tiny Bubbles 30
7 Full Circle 32
8 High Style 34
9 Cabled Cowlcho 36
10 Entrelac Blocks 39
11 Textured Lace 42
12 Sunny Slip Stitch 44
13 Slip-Stitch Style 46
14 Mosaic Diamonds 48
15 Openwork Flair 50
16 Wrap Party 53
17 Intarsia Ribs 56
18 Slip Stitch Stripes 60
19 Chevron Chic 62
20 Sea of Scallops 64
21 Check Mate 66
22 Tied in Knots 68
23 Sweet & Simple 70
24 Travel Time 72
25 Bobble Flowers 75
26 Ribs with a Twist 78
27 Ruffled Heathers 80
28 Bold Shoulders 82

29 Lattice Bliss 84
30 In the Loop 86
31 Bounty of Bobbles 88

32 Granny Square Glam 90
33 Ribbon Waves 93
34 Touch of Texture 96

35 Snug in Stripes 98
36 Waves of Lace 100
37 Windswept Cables 102
38 Bands of Bold 104
39 Frosted Flowers 106
40 Buttoned Up 108
41 Curled Up in Cables 111
42 Zigzag Ridges 114
43 Gather 'Round 116
44 Cozy Quilted 118
45 It's a Draw 120
46 Cables on the Edge 123
47 Horseshoe Cables 126
48 Budding Out 128
49 Pixelation 130
50 Woven with Care 132
51 Stepped-Up Stripes 134
52 Fishtail Cables 136
53 Zip It Up 138
54 Faux Cables 140
55 Braided Beauty 142
56 Pretty & Plaited 144
57 Honeycomb Heaven 146
58 Slouchy Stripes 148
59 Traveling Eyelets 150
60 Slipping Around 152

The Comfort of a Cowl

The popularity of knitted cowls has exploded, and it's no surprise: a cowl combines the warmth and style of a scarf with easy wearability and quick knitting. These fashion-forward accessories can be simple, straightforward knits or fun, challenging projects that are still quick to make. They're the perfect canvas for design elements of every type, from lace and cables to slip-stitch patterns and colorwork. The cowls featured in this book, the latest entry in the bestselling **60 Quick Knits** series, include all of the above. Each is made in Cascade Yarns' luxurious but affordable Cloud and Duo lines: super-soft blends of merino wool and baby alpaca in a cozy worsted-Aran weight that knits up in a jiffy.
Whether you're looking for a quick, satisfying project for yourself or an easy-but-elegant gift, you'll find a lot to love in these pages.

 To locate retailers that carry the **Cloud** and **Duo** lines of yarn, visit cascadeyarns.com.

Peruvian Gold

The perfect ingredient for a soft, warm cowl is amazing alpaca

Facts every knitter should
know about these gentle animals
and their incredible fiber

If you've never knit with alpaca or met one, it's time.

With their long necks, big eyes, and thick velvety noses, alpacas may look like creatures dreamed up by Dr. Seuss, especially just after shearing.

Ranchers in the United States and Canada began to import alpacas in the 1980s. The reasons for attraction were many: their loving temperament, easy care, and the availability of land. People in Canada and the United States scrambled to put their money down on this "huggable investment" and alpacas grew to become wildly popular during the 1990s and early 2000s.

At the height of the North American alpaca boom, alpacas commanded an average price of more than $25,000 a piece at auction. A handsome male Peruvian Royal Fawn set the world record when he was purchased for $600,000.

While prices have since fallen from their peak, the lovable alpaca remains popular for ranchers and knitters alike. Recently, the fashion industry has "discovered" what knitters already knew: alpaca is a beautiful and luxurious fiber.

Alpaca. The Back Story
While the modern alpaca was brought to North America in the 1980s, Paleontological records show that millions of years ago the ancestors of the alpaca called North America home. Moving from the New World to Old, these alpaca ancestors migrated to what is now Asia and Africa, via the Bering "landbridge." Others migrated south to South America, where they eventually became the alpaca.

Gentle and shy, alpaca are camelids, the same scientific family as camels, llamas, vicuñas, and guanacos. Camelids are distinguished by a few notable characteristics. All camelids are cud-chewers, but, unlike cows and goats, they have three-chambered stomachs. Cows and goats have four-chambered ones.

As a ruminant (cud chewer), alpacas have the ability to consume and survive upon low-quality forage. Watch an alpaca or camel chew and you'll notice that it masticates its food in a curious figure-eight pattern. After swallowing, an alpaca might burp up coarser bits for additional chewing. This is part of the digestive process known as rumination.

Compared to other four-legged animals like horses and cows, camelids are remarkably light on their feet. Behind their two hoof-like toenails is a large soft pad, not unlike that of a dog. This gives them a high-degree of sensory input from the ground, mak-

ing them extremely sure-footed. Due to this softer foot structure, camelids tend to have a lighter impact on their surroundings. They can even live in fragile high-altitude ecosystems without damaging the environment.

Another curious camelid feature is a penchant for spitting. Camels and llamas have gotten a bad rap for expressing displeasure by a well-aimed gob of cud. Typically, these slimy assaults are directed towards other animals when food is at issue, but as legions of YouTube videos attest, humans sometimes end up in the line of fire. While alpacas don't have the same cranky reputation as their larger cousins, breeders admit that from time to time "spit happens."

Camelids can be found in both the Eastern and Western Hemispheres. Dromedary camels (one hump) and Bactrian camels (two humps) are indigenous to the Middle East and parts of Africa and Asia. Though they are known for transporting people and gear (think Lawrence of Arabia), they are also wonderful fiber animals with incredibly soft down hidden beneath their guard hairs (remember camel hair coats?).

Native to South America, wild vicuña and guanaco herds still roam the high-altitude plains and slopes of the Andes Mountains; whereas

alpaca and llama are among the earliest domesticated species, having been tamed in the Peruvian Andes around 6,000 to 7,000 years ago.

Recent DNA research suggests that alpacas descended from the delicate vicuñas, which are prized for having some of the finest fiber in the world. It is said that only Incan royalty could wear fabric made from the precious fiber of this graceful animal. The Incas even used premium alpaca textiles as currency and guarded their fabric hoards like treasure. They revered these animals to the point that they even sacrificed them as offerings to their gods.

Today nearly 90 percent of the global alpaca herd is concentrated in Peru, which has around 3.6 million alpacas. Bolivia, the second largest producer, has a mere 9.5 percent of the world's alpacas. Chile, Argentina, the United States, Canada, New Zealand, Australia, also raise alpaca, but they don't even come close to the numbers of alpaca found in Peru or Bolivia.

There are as many as 1,400 breeds of sheep. By contrast, there are only two types of alpaca: the Huacaya and the Suri. The Huacaya is the variety you've probably seen on late night TV commercials extolling the alpaca lifestyle. About 90 percent of alpacas are Huacaya. They are woolier and look somewhat like long-necked standard poodles. They have shorter, slightly crimpy coats that

produce fiber with staple lengths in the two-to-six-inch range. The Suri, on the other hand, has a much longer, silkier fleece akin to soft dread locks. Their fiber is much longer with staple lengths that can run as long as 11 inches.

Alpaca rearing is considered a boutique enterprise. In the Andes it is a vital part of the livelihood for thousands of indigenous families, who rely on llamas and alpacas for survival. Women will often make and sell alpaca products, such as woven rugs or knitted hats and gloves, to tourists. However, most of the income to the alpaca herders comes from the sale of the unworked fiber. Raising their herds at elevations of 13,000 feet and higher, Andean herders, or alpaqueros, shear their animals annually. Local small-scale traders buy the alpaca wool from the alpaqueros and supply it to the processers in the city of Arequipa, where the majority of the world's alpaca fiber is processed.

A number of government-sponsored, non-profit, and socially conscious businesses currently work to both improve the quality of Peru's fiber and help the plight of subsistence farmers. As the producers of alpaca in Peru are small-scale family farmers, your purchase of alpaca impacts their well-being. The continued popularity of alpaca has seen the price of alpaca wool paid to the alpaqueros grow substantially over the past few years.

Now, about the yarn

Understandably, some call alpaca "the cashmere of the Andes." Both fibers are incredibly soft and luxurious.

While alpaca and cashmere are both soft, like wine grapes, the fibers have their own characteristics. Fibers are judged on many different qualities, with softness being only one of them. Others include luster, elasticity, and resistance to pilling. Beyond the differences between fibers from one type of animal to another, there are even differences between animal to animal, breeder to breeder, and even terroir to terroir.

Speaking of soft, Royal baby alpaca—the best of the best—is so sumptuous it can take your breath away. The terms "royal" and "baby," however, have nothing to do with an animal's age or pedigree, but instead are a classification related to the fiber's quality or diameter in microns.

A lower micron count equals slimmer, softer fibers. To give you a sense of scale, a human hair can range from 50 to about 120 microns in diameter. Those with finer manes are on the lower end of the spectrum, while those with coarser or curly thatches are on the other. Cashmere runs between 14 to 19 microns, merino ranges from 11.5 to 25 microns, and alpaca can fall anywhere from 15 to 35 microns. In Peru, industrial processors employ a subjective grading system

to sort and classify alpaca fiber. Using their highly trained eyes and hands, graders sort alpaca fibers into general classifications. These classifications may vary from company to company, but royal baby or royal alpaca typically comes in at 19 or fewer microns, baby alpaca is approximately 22.5 microns, and superfine alpaca hovers around 25.5 microns.

The structure of alpaca fiber can make alpaca feel even softer than wool of the same micron count. Examine wool under a microscope and you'll notice that it looks like tree bark with the scales on its surface creating a rough, uneven texture. Alpaca fibers are scaly, too, but less so, making it silkier to the touch even if its diameter is thicker.

Alpacas also don't produce lanolin, which is the greasy wax secreted by the sebaceous glands of sheep. Because lanolin is a potential allergen, some people who are sensitive to wool might find alpaca to be an enjoyable alternative. Not only is it smoother in texture, but some even go so far as to say that alpaca is hypoallergenic.

Alpaca fiber has many other laudable qualities. Want a fiber that pills less? Alpaca is stronger and more abrasion resistant than wool or cashmere. Because it has a hollow core, it makes an incredible lightweight insulation that stays warm even when wet. It also felts (although not as easily as wool) and comes in an almost infinite variety of natural colors that range from inky black to creamy white. Plus, it takes dye beautifully, though colors tend to come out lighter and less intense than dyed wool.

Alpaca sounds like the answer to all your fiber hopes and dreams, doesn't it? But alpaca has its own idiosyncrasies. Whereas wool is much vaunted for its elasticity or memory, giving garments the ability to retain their shape, a 100-percent alpaca yarn possesses very little of that springy quality. Knit a sweater in a chunky alpaca yarn and it might droop over time. But knit a shawl in a lace or fingering weight and watch alpaca's drape open up the pattern like a butterfly wing.

Alpaca fiber, though, plays well with others. A marriage of wool and alpaca gives you the best of all possible worlds. Imbued with the sheen and strength of alpaca, a good alpaca-wool-blend yarn also has the down-to-earth spunk and bounce of wool. The reason why the alpaca yarns in this book were blended with merino was to give the yarn more elasticity than a pure alpaca fiber.

Do indulge in this exotic fiber. And if you have the opportunity to visit an alpaca ranch, see if you can score a kiss from one of these adorable creatures. You'll never be the same.

Alpaca by the numbers

- 87% of the world's alpaca population lives in Peru.

- 9.5% are raised in Bolivia.

- 4.2 million is the approximate number of the global alpaca herd.

- $600,000 is the highest price ever paid for an alpaca, an Accoyo male by the name of Peruvian Royal Fawn.

- 4 to 6 lbs represents the average amount of fiber one animal produces in a year.

- 18 to 20 years is the typical alpaca lifespan.

- 52 natural colors are the number of classified hues on the market in Peru. In the United States that number is 16.

4 Gorgeous
Gathers
(Page 25)

Projects

Riches of Ribs

Holding two strands of yarn together makes a simple
oversized ribbed cowl even more stylishly chunky.

DESIGNED AUDREY DRYSDALE

Knitted Measurements
Circumference 39"/99cm
Length 17"/43cm

Materials
▪ 6 3½oz/100g hanks (each approx
164yd/150m) of Cascade Yarns *Cloud*
(merino wool/baby alpaca) in
#2113 lilac (4)
▪ Size 10 ½ (6.5mm) circular needle,
29"/74cm long, *or size to obtain gauge*
▪ Stitch marker

Stitch Glossary
p1-b Purl 1 in the rnd below.

Fisherman's Rib
(over an even number of sts)
Rnd 1 Knit.
Rnd 2 *K1, p1-b; rep from * around.
Rep rnds 1 and 2 for fisherman's rib.

Cowl
With 2 strands of yarn held tog, cast on
110 sts. Join, taking care not to twist sts,
and place marker for beg of rnd.
Work in fisherman's rib until piece measures
17"/43cm from beg, end with a rnd 2.
Bind off loosely.▪

Gauge
11 sts and 23 rnds to 4"/10cm over fisherman's rib using size 10 ½ (6.5mm) needle and 2 strands of yarn held tog.
Take time to check gauge.

Leaning Tower

A terrifically tall cowl with an easy pattern of diagonal ridges gathers when worn for super-cozy warmth.

DESIGNED BY CHERI ESPER

■■□□

Knitted Measurements
Circumference 20"/51cm
Length 19"/48cm

Materials
■ 2 3½oz/100g hanks (each approx 197yd/180m) of Cascade Yarns *Eco Duo* (baby alpaca/merino wool) in #1705 vanilla (④)
■ Size 9 (5.5mm) circular needle, 16"/40cm long, *or size to obtain gauge*
■ Stitch marker

Rnd 1 [K10, p10] 4 times.
Rnd 2 Remove marker, k1, replace marker, [p10, k10] 4 times.
Rnd 3 [P10, k10] 4 times.
Rnd 4 Remove marker, p1, replace marker, [k10, p10] 4 times.
Rep rnds 1–4 for pat st until cowl measures approx 19"/48cm or desired length. Bind off.■

Note
Round shifts 1 stitch to the left at the beginning of rounds 2 and 4.

Cowl
Cast on 80 sts. Join, taking care not to twist sts, and place marker for beg of rnd.

Gauge
16 sts and 28 rnds to 4"/10cm over pat st using size 9 (5.5mm) needle.
Take time to check gauge.

Cable & Bobble Combo

Chunky cables and bobbles encircle a cozy cowl
that's a study in three-dimensional design.

DESIGNED BY LINDA MEDINA

Knitted Measurements
Circumference 30"/76cm
Width 10"/25.5cm

Materials
▨ 3 3½oz/100g hanks (each approx
164yd/150m) of Cascade Yarns *Cloud*
(merino wool/alpaca) in #2128
tarragon (4)
▨ One pair size 10 (6mm) needles
or size to obtain gauge
▨ One each sizes 7 and 8 (4.5 and 5mm)
circular needles, 24"/60cm long
▨ Stitch markers
▨ Cable needle (cn)
▨ Size K/10½ (6.5mm) crochet hook and
scrap yarn of similar weight to working
yarn for provisional cast-on

Stitch Glossary
MB (make bobble) Knit into the front,
back, and front of next st, [turn, k3] 3
times, turn, SK2P.
3-st RC Sl 1 st to cn, hold to *back,* k2,
k1 from cn.
3-st LPC Sl 2 sts to cn, hold to *front,* p1,
k2 from cn.
5-st RPC Sl 2 sts to cn, hold to *back,* k3,
p2 from cn.
5-st LPC Sl 3 sts to cn, hold to *front* p2,
k3 from cn.
6-st RC Sl 3 sts to cn, hold to *back,* k3,
k3 from cn.

Provisional Cast-On
Using scrap yarn and crochet hook, ch
the number of sts to cast on plus a few
extra. Cut a tail and pull the tail through
the last chain. With knitting needle and
yarn, pick up and knit the stated number
of sts through the "purl bumps" on the
back of the chain. To remove scrap yarn
chain, when instructed, pull out the tail
from the last crochet stitch. Gently and
slowly pull on the tail to unravel the crochet stitches, carefully placing each released knit stitch on a needle.

Cowl
With size 10 (6mm) needles, cast on 50
sts using provisional cast-on method.
Work rows 1–12 of chart 15 times.
Carefully remove provisional cast-on and
place live sts on needle. Graft ends
together.

Gauge
25 sts and 24 rows to 4"/10cm over chart pat using size 10 (6mm) needles.
Take time to check gauge.

Cable & Bobble Combo

EDGING

With RS facing and larger circular needle, pick up and k 160 sts evenly along one long edge of cowl. Join and place marker for beg of rnd.

Rnd 1 *K1, p1; rep from * around.
Rep rnd 1 for k1, p1 rib for 4 rnds more. With smaller circular needle, bind off in rib.
Rep for opposite edge.■

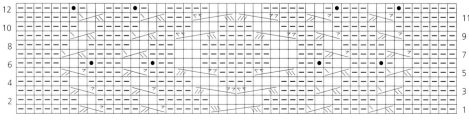

50 sts

STITCH KEY

☐ k on RS, p on WS

— p on RS, k on WS

● make bobble (MB)

3-st RC

3-st LPC

5-st RPC

5-st LPC

6-st RC

Gorgeous Gathers

Gathered welts form a ruched effect that's equally lovely knitted in solid or variegated hues.

DESIGNED BY ERICA SCHLUETER

Knitted Measurements
Circumference 23"/58.5cm
Length 9"/23cm

Materials
▓ 2 3½oz/100g hanks (each approx 197yd/180m) of Cascade Yarns *Eco Duo* (baby alpaca/merino wool) in #1703 storm (▓4▓)
▓ Size 9 (5.5mm) circular needle, 16"/40cm long, *or size to obtain gauge*
▓ One size 8 (5mm) double-pointed needle (dpn)
▓ Size J/10 (6mm) crochet hook
▓ Stitch marker

Making a Welt
With dpn, working on WS of work, pick up 12 sts in the last purl row 12 rows below, just below the first row of wedge section. Hold 12 picked-up sts behind working needle and *k next st on working needle tog with next st on dpn; rep from * until 12 sts are joined.

Cowl
Cast on 90 sts. Join, taking care not to twist sts, and place marker for beg of rnd.
Knit 5 rnds.

BEG WELT PATTERN
Rnd 1 K4, *p1, k17, rep from * to last 14 sts, p1, k13.
Rnd 2 K4, *p2, k16, rep from * to last 14 sts, p2, k12.
Rnd 3 K4, *p3, k15, rep from * to last 14 sts, p3, k11.
Rnd 4 K4, *p4, k14, rep from * to last 14 sts, p4, k10.
Rnd 5 K4, *p5, k13, rep from * to last 14 sts, p5, k9.
Rnd 6 K4, *p6, k12, rep from * to last 14 sts, p6, k8.
Rnd 7 K4, *p7, k11, rep from * to last 14 sts, p7, k7.
Rnd 8 K4, *p8, k10, rep from * to last 14 sts, p8, k6.
Rnd 9 K4, *p9, k9, rep from * to last 14 sts, p9, k5.
Rnd 10 K4, *p10, k8, rep from * to last 14 sts, p10, k4.
Rnd 11 K4, *p11, k7, rep from * to last 14 sts, p11, k3.
Rnd 12 K4, *p12, k6 rep from * to last

Gauge
17 sts and 24 rows to 4"/10cm over St st using size 9 (5.5mm) needles.
Take time to check gauge.

Gorgeous Gathers

14 sts, p12, k2.

Rnd 13 K4, *make welt over 12 sts, k6, rep from * to last 14 sts, make welt over 12 sts, k2.

Rnd 14 Knit.

Rnd 15 *K17, p1, rep from * around.

Rnd 16 *K16, p2, rep from * around.

Rnd 17 *K15, p3, rep from * around.

Rnd 18 *K14, p4, rep from * around.

Rnd 19 *K13, p5, rep from * around.

Rnd 20 *K12, p6, rep from * around.

Rnd 21 *K11, p7, rep from * around.

Rnd 22 *K10, p8, rep from * around.

Rnd 23 *K9, p9, rep from * around.

Rnd 24 *K8, p10, rep from * around.

Rnd 25 *K7, p11, rep from * around.

Rnd 26 *K6, p12, rep from * around.

Rnd 27 *K6, make welt over 12 stitches, rep from * around.

Rep rows 1-27 twice more.

Knit 5 rnds. Bind off.■

Fetching Feather & Fan

Show off a classic lace motif by alternating with Stockinette stitch bands in a dramatically long loop.

DESIGNED BY ANASTASIA BLAES

Knitted Measurements
Circumference 56"/142cm
Length 7"/18cm

Materials
▪ 2 3½oz/100g hanks (each approx 197yd/180m) of Cascade Yarns *Highland Duo* (baby alpaca/merino wool) in #2310 honey (4)
▪ Size 8 (5mm) circular needle, 40"/100cm long, *or size to obtain gauge*
▪ Stitch markers

BEG PATTERN STITCH
Rnds 1, 3, 5, and 7 *[Ssk] twice, yo, [k1, yo] 3 times, [k2tog] twice; rep from * around.
Rnds 2, 4, and 6 Knit.
Rnd 8 Purl.
Rnds 9–14 Knit.
Rnd 15 Purl.
Rep rnds 1–15 once more, then rep rnds 1–8 once.
Knit 1 rnd, purl 1 rnd. Bind off loosely knitwise.

Finishing
Block lightly to measurements. ▪

Cowl
Cast on 264 sts. Join, taking care not to twist sts, and place marker for beg of rnd.
[Knit 1 rnd, purl 1 rnd] twice.

Gauge
19 sts and 23 rnds to 4"/10cm over pat st using size 8 (5mm) needle.
Take time to check gauge.

6

Tiny Bubbles

A fun cocoon stitch pattern gathers stitches
into a soft sand snuggly parade of poufs.

DESIGNED BY ASHLEY RAO

Knitted Measurements
Circumference 26"/66cm
Length 10½"/26.5cm

Materials
▪ 3 3½oz/100g hanks (each approx
164yd/150m) of Cascade Yarns *Eco
Cloud* (merino wool/baby alpaca) in
#1804 bunny (4)
▪ Size 10 (6mm) circular needle,
24"/60cm long, *or size to obtain gauge*
▪ Stitch marker

Stitch Glossary
M1 p-st Insert needle from front to back
under the strand between the last st
worked and the next st on the LH needle. Purl into the back loop to twist the st.

Cocoon Stitch
(multiple of 8 sts)
Rnds 1 and 2 *K1, p1, k1, p5; rep from
* around.
Rnd 3 *K1, M1 p-st, (p1, k1, p1) in next
st, M1 p-st, k1, k5tog; rep from *
around.
Rnds 4–8 *K1, p5, k1, p1; rep from *
around.
Rnd 9 *K1, k5tog, k1, M1 p-st, (p1, k1,
p1) in next st, M1 p-st; rep from *
around.
Rnds 10–12 *K1, p1, k1, p5; rep from *
around.
Rep rnds 1–12 for cocoon stitch.

Cowl
Cast on 120 sts. Join, taking care not to
twist sts, and place marker for beg of
rnd. Work rnds 1–12 of cocoon stitch 5
times, then work rnds 1–3 once more.

SHORT-ROW BIND-OFF
Next rnd K1, *p5, turn work, k5, turn
work, [p1, pass st on RH needle over last
st worked (pso)] 5 times, k1, pso, p1,
pso, k1, pso; rep from * to last st, fasten
off last st.

Finishing
Block lightly to measurements. ▪

Gauge
18 sts and 24 rnds to 4"/10cm over cocoon st using size 10 (6mm) needle.
Take time to check gauge.

Full Circle

A creative coin stitch forms oversized polka dots, kept in line
by a garter stitch border and I-cord edging.

DESIGNED BY KATHY NORTH

Knitted Measurements
Circumference 26"/66cm
Length 8"/20.5cm

Materials
▧ 1 3½oz/100g hank (each approx
197yd/180m) of Cascade Yarns *Highland
Duo* (baby alpaca/merino wool) each in
#2315 deep teal (MC) and #2323 green
spruce (CC) (❹)
▧ Size 10 (6mm) circular needle,
24"/60cm long, *or size to obtain gauge*
▧ Two size 10 (6mm) double-pointed
needles (dpns)
▧ Size J/10 (6mm) crochet hook and
scrap yarn for provisional cast-on
▧ Stitch marker

Notes
Carry unused color loosely up inside
work. When changing colors, bring new
color up under old color to avoid holes in
work.

Provisional Cast-On
Using scrap yarn and crochet hook, chain
the number of sts to cast on, plus a few
extra. Cut a tail and pull the tail through
the last chain. With knitting needle and
yarn, pick up and knit the stated number
of sts through the "purl bumps" on the
back of the chain. To remove scrap chain,
when instructed, pull out the tail from the
last crochet st. Gently and slowly pull on
the tail to unravel the crochet sts, carefully
placing each released knit st on a needle.

Coin Stitch Pattern
(multiple of 4 sts)
Rnd 1 With MC, knit.
Rnds 2–5 With CC, knit.
Rnd 6 With MC, *k3, drop next st and
unravel 4 rows down, insert RH needle
from front to back into MC st in 5th row
below and knit, gathering 4 loose
strands in st; rep from * around.
Rnd 7 With MC, knit.
Rnds 8–11 With CC, knit.
Rnd 12 With MC, k1, *drop next st and
unravel 4 rows down, insert RH needle
from front to back into MC st in 5th row
below and knit, gathering 4 loose
strands in st, k3; rep from * around,
ending last rep k2.
Rep rnds 1–12 for coin stitch pat.

Cowl
With MC, loosely cast on 96 sts using provisional cast-on. Join, taking care not to
twist sts, and place marker for beg of rnd.
With MC, knit 1 rnd, purl 1 rnd. With
CC, knit 1 rnd, purl 1 rnd, knit 2 rnds.
Work rnds 1–12 of coin stitch 3 times,
then work rnds 1–7 once more.
With CC, knit 2 rnds, purl 1 rnd, knit 1
rnd. With MC, knit 1 rnd, purl 1 rnd,
knit 1 rnd. Do *not* bind off.

Finishing
APPLIED I-CORD EDGING
With MC and dpn, cast on 4 sts. K3, k
last st on dpn tog with first st on circular
needle, *do not turn, slide sts back to
beg of needle to work next row from RS,
k3, ssk (working last st on dpn tog with
next st on circular needle); rep from *
around until all sts from circular needle
have been joined to edging. Bind off rem
4 sts, sew first and last rows of I-cord
edging tog.
Carefully remove provisional cast-on
from cast-on edge and work applied
I-cord edging in the same way.∎

Gauges
16 sts and 22 rnds to 4"/10cm over St st using size 10 (6mm) needles.
15 sts and 28 rnds to 4"/10cm over coin stitch pat using size 10 (6mm) needles. *Take time to check gauges.*

High Style

Stay warm and look cool with a chunky cabled cowl that holds its shape to keep out the chill.

DESIGNED BY ANNE JONES

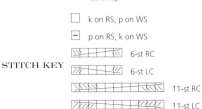

Knitted Measurements
Circumference 22"/56cm
Length 6½"/16.5cm

Materials
■ 2 3½oz/100g hanks (each approx 164yd/150m) of Cascade Yarns *Cloud* (merino wool/baby alpaca) in #2120 true blue (4)
■ One each sizes 6 and 8 (4 and 5mm) circular needles, 16"/40cm long, *or size to obtain gauge*
■ Cable needle (cn)
■ Stitch markers

Stitch Glossary
6-st RC Sl 3 sts to cn, hold to *back*, k3, k3 from cn.
6-st LC Sl 3 sts to cn, hold to *front*, k3, k3 from cn.
11-st RC Sl 6 sts to cn, hold to *back*, k5, k6 from cn.
11-st LC Sl 5 sts to cn, hold to *front*, k6, k5 from cn.

Cowl
With smaller needle, cast on 130 sts. Join, taking care not to twist sts, and

place marker for beg of rnd. Purl 4 rnds. Change to larger needle.

BEG CHART
Rnd 1 Work 26-st chart rep 5 times. Cont to work chart in this manner through rnd 39.

Change to smaller needle. Purl 4 rnds. Bind off purlwise.

Finishing
Block to measurements. ■

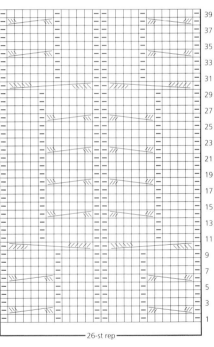

— 26-st rep —

☐ k on RS, p on WS

⊟ p on RS, k on WS

6-st RC

6-st LC

STITCH KEY

11-st RC

11-st LC

Gauge
24 sts and 28 rnds to 4"/10cm over chart pat using size 8 (5mm) needle.
Take time to check gauge.

9

Cabled Cowlcho

Cowl meets poncho in a stunning Aran piece to wear over your coat or as its own outerwear.

DESIGNED BY AUDREY DRYSDALE

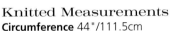

Knitted Measurements
Circumference 44"/111.5cm
Length 17"/43cm

Materials
■ 6 3½oz/100g hanks (each approx 164yd/150m) of Cascade Yarns *Eco Cloud* (merino wool/baby alpaca) in #1809 dove gray (4)
■ One pair size 8 (5mm) needles, *or size to obtain gauge*
■ Size 8 (5mm) circular needle, 24"/60cm long
■ Cable needle (cn)
■ Stitch markers

Stitch Glossary
3-st RPC Sl 1 st to cn, hold to *back*, k2, p1 from cn.
3-st LPC Sl 2 sts to cn, hold to *front*, p1, k2 from cn.
5-st RC Sl 3 sts to cn, hold to *back*, k2, sl purl st from cn to LH needle, p1, then k2 from cn.
6-st RC Sl 3 sts to cn, hold to *back*, k3, k3 from cn.
6-st LC Sl 3 sts to cn, hold to *front*, k3, k3 from cn.
6-st RPC Sl 4 sts to cn, hold to *back*, k2, sl 2 purl sts from cn to LH needle, p2, then k2 from cn.
6-st LPC Sl 4 sts to cn, hold to front, k2, sl 2 purl sts from cn to LH needle, p2, then k2 from cn.

Note
Front and back cable pieces are worked from side to side. After sides are sewn, collar is picked up and worked in the round.

Back
Cast on 38 sts.
Set-up row (WS) K5, [p3, M1 p-st] twice, p1, k7, p2, k1, p2, k7, [p3, M1 p-st] twice, p1—42 sts.

BEG CHARTS AND SHAPING
Row 1 (RS) Cast on 2 sts, p2 (rev St st), place marker (pm), work cable A over 9 sts, pm, work cable B over 19 sts, pm, work cable A over 9 sts, p2 (rev St st), k3 (garter st selvage sts)—44 sts.
Row 2 (WS) K3 (garter st selvage sts),

Gauge
18 sts and 24 rows to 4"/10cm over St st using size 8 (5mm) needles.
Take time to check gauge.

Cabled Cowlcho

CABLE A

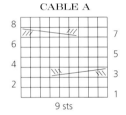

9 sts

CABLE C

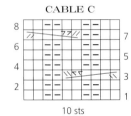

10 sts

CABLE B

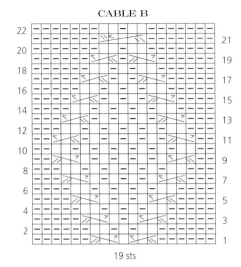

19 sts

STITCH KEY

☐ k on RS, p on WS

⊟ p on RS, k on WS

3-st RPC

3-st LPC

5-st RPC

6-st RC

6-st LC

6-st RPC

6-st LPC

k2 (rev St st), work in cable pats as established to last 2 sts, k2 (rev St st).
Cont in pats as established, cast on 2 sts at beg of RS rows 5 times more, working cast-on sts into cable C (k2, p2, k2, p2, k2)—54 sts.
Row 13 (RS) Cast on 2 sts, p2 (rev St st), beg with row 7, work cable C over 10 sts, pm, work cables as established to last 5 sts, p2, k3—56 sts.
Cont in pats as established, cast on 2 sts at beg of RS rows 5 times more, working cast-on sts into cable C (k2, p2, k2, p2, k2)—66 sts.
Row 25 (RS) Cast on 2 sts, p2 (rev St st), beg with row 7, work cable C over 10 sts, pm, work cables as established to last 5 sts, p2, k3—68 sts.
Cont in pats as established until 22 rows of cable B have been worked 5 times, then work rows 1–18 once more.
Cont in pats, bind off 2 sts at beg of next 13 RS rows. Work 1 WS row.
Bind off, working 2 decreases evenly across each cable A.

Front
Work same as for back.

Finishing
Block pieces lightly to measurements. Sew side seams.

COLLAR
With RS facing and circular needle, beg at side seam, pick up and k 140 sts evenly around neck edge. Join and place marker for beg of rnd.
Rnds 1 and 2 *K2, p2; rep from * around.
Rnds 3 and 4 *P2, k2; rep from * around.
Rep rnds 1–4 until collar measures 7½"/19cm, end with a rnd 2 or 4. Bind off knitwise. ■

Entrelac Blocks

If you've never explored the woven look of entrelac, this ridge stitch cowl would make a great first project.

DESIGNED BY ROSEMARY DRYSDALE

◼◼◼▢

Knitted Measurements
Circumference 30"/76cm
Length 8½"/21.5cm

Materials
■ 1 3½oz/100g hank (each approx 164yd/150m) of Cascade Yarns *Cloud* (merino wool/baby alpaca) each in #2114 plum (A) and #2130 anemone (B) **(4)**
■ Size 9 (5.5mm) circular needle, 24"/60cm long, *or size to obtain gauge*
■ Stitch marker

Ridge Stitch on RS
Row 1 (RS) Knit.
Row 2 Purl.
Ridge row 3 Purl.
Row 4 Purl.
Rep rows 1–4 for ridge st on RS.

Ridge Stitch on WS
Row 1 (WS) Purl.
Row 2 Purl.
Ridge row 3 Purl.
Row 4 Knit.
Rep rows 1–4 for ridge st on WS.

Short Row Wrap & Turn (w&t)
on RS row (on WS row)
1) Wyib (wyif), sl next st purlwise.
2) Move yarn between the needles to the front (back).
3) Sl the same st back to LH needle. Turn work. One st is wrapped.

4) When working the wrapped st, insert RH needle under the wrap and work it tog with the corresponding st on needle.

Cowl
With A, cast on 96 sts. Join, taking care not to twist sts and place marker for beg of rnd.
Knit 1 rnd, purl 1 rnd. Join B and knit 1 rnd, purl 1 rnd.
Work in entrelac pat as foll:

BASE TRIANGLES
Work with A as foll:
***Row 1 (RS)** K1, turn.
Row 2 (WS) P1, turn.
Row 3 K2, turn.
Row 4 P2, turn.
Row 5 K3, turn.
Row 6 P3, turn.
Row 7 K4, turn.
Row 8 P4, turn.
Row 9 K5, turn.
Row 10 P5, turn.
Row 11 K6, turn.
Row 12 P6, turn.
Row 13 K7, turn.
Row 14 P7, turn.

Gauge
18 sts and 32 rows to 4"/10cm over ridge st using size 9 (5.5mm) needle.
Take time to check gauge.

Row 15 K8, do *not* turn—1 triangle made.
Rep from * for 11 more triangles—12 triangles made. Turn work to WS.

WS RECTANGLES
**With WS facing and B, using RH needle, pick up and p 8 sts evenly down left edge of first base triangle, turn.
Beg with row 1, work in ridge st on RS as foll:

Next row (RS) P8, turn.
*****Next row (WS)** P7, p2tog (with last st of rectangle and first st of base triangle), turn.

Next row (RS) K8, turn.
Rep from *, keeping in ridge st, until all sts from base triangle are worked, end with last WS row as foll: P7, p2tog (8 sts B on RH needle). Do *not* turn.**
Rep from ** to ** for 11 more WS rectangles.

RS RECTANGLES
*****With RS facing and A, using RH needle, pick up and k 8 sts evenly down left edge of first WS rectangle, turn.
Beg with row 1, work in ridge st on WS as foll:
*****Next row (WS)** P8, turn.
Row 2 P7, p2tog (with last st of rectan-

gle and first st of next triangle/rectangle), turn.*
Rep from * to * until all sts from WS rectangle are worked, do *not* turn at end of last RS row.***
Rep from *** to *** until 12 RS rectangles have been made, turn at end of last RS row.
Work another set of 12 WS rectangles, 12 RS rectangles, and 12 WS rectangles.

END TRIANGLES
Work triangles with A as foll:
*****Next row (RS)** With A, pick up and k 8 sts evenly down left edge of first WS rectangle, turn.
Row 1 (WS) P7, w&t.
Row 2 (RS) K6, ssk, turn.
Row 3 P6, w&t.
Row 4 K5, ssk, turn.
Row 5 P5, w&t.
Row 6 K4, ssk, turn.
Row 7 P4, w&t.
Row 8 K3, ssk, turn.
Row 9 P3, w&t.
Row 10 K2, ssk, turn.
Row 11 P2, w&t.
Row 12 K1, ssk, turn.
Row 13 P1, w&t.
Row 14 Slip 1, k2tog, psso, do *not* turn.
Rep from * until 12 end triangles have been made.
With B, knit 1 rnd, purl 1 rnd.
With A, knit 1 rnd, purl 1 rnd, bind off knitwise.■

Textured Lace

An earthy neutral is the perfect canvas for a combination of lace and textured motifs.

DESIGNED BY ANNIKEN ALLIS

Knitted Measurements
Circumference 20"/51cm
Length 11"/28cm

Materials
▪ 1 3½oz//100g hank (each approx 197yd/180m) of Cascade Yarns *Eco Highland Duo* (baby alpaca/merino wool) in #2113 lilac (**4**)
▪ Size 10 (6mm) circular needle, 16"/40cm long, *or size to obtain gauge*
▪ Stitch marker

Lace Pattern
(multiple of 10 sts)
Rnd 1 Knit.
Rnd 2 Purl.
Rnd 3 Knit.
Rnd 4 Purl.
Rnd 5 *Yo, k3, S2KP, k3, yo, k1; rep from * around.
Rnds 6, 8, 10, 12, 14, 16, and 18 Knit.
Rnd 7 *K1, yo, k2, S2KP, k2, yo, k2; rep from * around.
Rnd 9 *K2, yo, k1, S2KP, k1, yo, k3; rep from * around.
Rnd 11 *K3, yo, S2KP, yo, k4; rep from * around.

Rnd 13 *Yo, ssk, k5, k2tog, yo, k1; rep from * around.
Rnd 15 *K1, yo, ssk, yo, S2KP, yo, k2tog, yo, k2; rep from * around.
Rnd 7 *K2, yo, ssk, k1, k2tog, yo, k3; rep from * around.
Rnd 19 *K3, yo, S2KP, yo, k4; rep from * around.

Rep rnds 1–19 for lace pat.

Note
Lace pattern can be worked from text *or* chart.

Cowl
Cast on 80 sts. Join, being careful not to twist sts, and place marker for beg of rnds.

BEG LACE PATTERN
Next rnd Work 10-st rep 8 times around. Cont to work in this manner until rnd 19 is complete. Rep rnds 1–19 twice more, then rnds 1–4 once. Bind off. Block if necessary. ▪

LACE PATTERN

			O	⅄	O				19
		O	◿		⅄	O			17
		O	◿	O	⅄	O	⅄	O		15
	O	◿					⅄	O	13
			O	⅄	O				11
		O		⅄		O			9
		O		⅄		O			7
	O			⅄			O		5
									3
									1

10-st rep

STITCH KEY
☐ k on RS, p on WS
⊟ p on RS, k on WS
◿ k2tog
⍀ ssk
O yo
⅄ S2KP

Gauge
16 sts and 22 rnds to 4"/10cm over pat st using size 10 (6mm) needle.
Take time to check gauge.

Sunny Slip Stitch

A simple slip stitch checked pattern catches the eye
with an oversized shape and bright hues.

DESIGNED BY JACQUELINE VAN DILLEN

Knitted Measurements
Circumference 60"/152cm
Width 11"/28cm

Materials
▪ 3 3½oz/100g hanks (each approx
164yd/150m) of Cascade Yarns *Cloud*
(merino wool/baby alpaca) in #2104
golden (▨)
▪ 2 3½oz/100g hanks (each approx
164yd/150m) of Cascade Yarns *Eco
Cloud* (merino wool/baby alpaca) in
#1809 dove gray (CC) (▨)
▪ One pair size 10 (6mm) needles *or size
to obtain gauge*
▪ Stitch markers

Right Border Pattern
(over 6 sts with MC only)
Row 1 (RS) Sl 1 st knitwise wyib, [k1,
p1] twice, k1.
Row 2 [P1, k1] twice, p2.
Rep rows 1 and 2 for right border pat.

Left Border Pattern
(over 6 sts with MC only)

Row 1 (RS) [K1, p1] 3 times.
Row 2 Sl 1 st knitwise wyif, [p1, k1]
twice, p1.
Rep rows 1 and 2 for left border pat.

Slip Stitch Pattern
(over an odd number of sts)
Row 1 (RS) With MC, knit.

Row 2 With MC, purl.
Row 3 With CC, k1, *sl 1 wyib, k1; rep
from * to end.
Row 4 With CC, *k1, sl 1 wyif; rep from *,
end k1.
Rows 5 and 6 Rep rows 1 and 2.
Row 7 With CC, sl 1 wyib, *k1, sl 1
wyib; rep from * to end.
Row 8 With CC, *sl 1 wyif, k1; rep from *,
end sl 1 wyif.
Rep rows 1–8 for slip st pat.

Cowl
With MC, cast on 55 sts.
Row 1 (RS) Work 6 sts in right border
pat, place marker (pm), work row 1 of
slip st pat over 43 sts, pm, work 6 sts in
left border pat.
Cont in pats as established until piece
measures 60"/152cm from beg, measur-
ing at center of work (side borders pull
in slightly), and ending with a sl st pat
row 4 or 8.
With MC, bind off.
Sew bound-off edge to cast-on edge.■

Gauge
18 sts and 30 rows to 4"/10cm over slip stitch pat using size 10 (6mm) needles.
Take time to check gauge.

13

Slip-Stitch Style

A tweedy slip-stitch pattern evokes a modern vintage look in a buttoned-up neckwarmer.

DESIGNED BY ANNE HATCHER

Knitted Measurements
Circumference (buttoned) 22"/56cm
Length 9½"/24cm

Materials
■ 1 3½oz/100g hank (each approx 164yd/150m) of Cascade Yarns *Eco Cloud* (merino wool/baby alpaca) each in #1804 bunny (A) and #1803 fawn (B) (**4**)
■ Size 9 (5.5mm) circular needle, 24"/60cm long, *or size to obtain gauge*
■ Four ⅞"/22mm buttons

Notes
1) Circular needle is used to accommodate large number of stitches, do *not* join.
2) Carry color not in use along side of work.

Cowl
With A, cast on 103 sts. Purl 3 rows.

BEG SLIP STITCH PATTERN
Row 1 (WS) With B, p1, sl 1 wyib, *p3,

sl 1 wyib; rep from * to last st, p1.
Row 2 (RS) With B, k1, sl 1 wyib, *k3, sl 1 wyib; rep from * to last st, k1.
Row 3 With A, p3, *sl 1 wyib, p3; rep from * to end.
Row 4 With A, k3, *sl 1 wyib, k3; rep from * to end.
Rep rows 1–4 for slip stitch pat until

piece measures approx 9"/23cm from beg, end with a row 1 of pat. Do *not* turn work, slide sts to opposite side to work a WS row with A. With A, k 3 rows. With A, bind off.

BUTTON BAND
With RS facing and A, pick up and k 44 sts evenly along one short edge. Knit 2 rows. Bind off knitwise.

BUTTONHOLE BAND
With RS facing and A, pick up and k 44 sts evenly along opposite short edge.
Buttonhole row (WS) K3, [bind off 2 sts, k until there are 10 sts worked from bind-off] 3 times, bind off 2 sts, k to end.
Next row (RS) Knit, casting on 2 sts over bound-off sts.
Bind off knitwise.

Finishing
Block lightly to measurements. Sew buttons to button band opposite buttonholes. ■

Gauge
20 sts and 28 rows to 4"/10cm over slip stitch pat using size 9 (5.5mm) needle.
Take time to check gauge.

14

Mosaic Diamonds

Geometric colorwork steals the show in a mosaic-style pattern of diamonds and dots.

DESIGNED BY ANN MCDONALD KELLY

Knitted Measurements
Circumference 29"/73.5cm
Length 11"/28cm

Materials
■ 1 3½oz/100g hank (each approx 164yd/150m) of Cascade Yarns *Cloud* (merino wool/baby alpaca) each in #2122 lupin (A) and #2128 tarragon (B)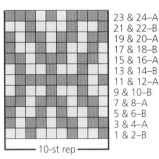
■ Size 8 (5mm) circular needle, 24"/60cm long, *or size to obtain gauge*
■ Stitch marker

Cowl
With A, cast on 130 sts. Join, taking care not to twist sts, and place marker for beg of rnd.
Purl 1 rnd, knit 1 rnd, purl 1 rnd.

BEG CHART
Work rnds 1–24 of chart 3 times, then work rnds 1–10 once more.
With A, purl 1 rnd, knit 1 rnd, purl 1 rnd. Bind off knitwise.

Finishing
Block lightly to measurements. ■

23 & 24–A
21 & 22–B
19 & 20–A
17 & 18–B
15 & 16–A
13 & 14–B
11 & 12–A
9 & 10–B
7 & 8–A
5 & 6–B
3 & 4–A
1 & 2–B

— 10-st rep —

COLOR KEY

■ Lupin (A)

□ Tarragon (B)

Notes
1) One row of chart represents two rounds of knitting. Read all rounds from right to left. Only one color is worked over 2 rounds, slipping the other color purlwise wyib. The color for each pair of rounds is indicated on the right side of chart.
2) Chart is worked in St st (knit every round).
3) Carry yarn not in use loosely up inside of work, twisting at beg of round to avoid holes in work.

Gauge
18 sts and 34 rnds to 4"/10cm over chart pat using size 8 (5mm) needles.
Take time to check gauge.

Openwork Flair

A pattern of eyelets created by gathering wrapped stitches adds lightness to a long, flared cowl.

DESIGNED BY LARS RAINS

Knitted Measurements
Circumference at neck edge 45"/114cm
Circumference at lower edge
74"/188cm
Length 10"/25.5cm

Materials
■ 3 3½oz/100g hanks (each approx 197yd/180m) of Cascade Yarns *Highland Duo* (baby alpaca/merino wool) in #2305 purple orchid (▨)
■ Size 8 (5mm) circular needle, 40"/100cm long, *or size to obtain gauge*
■ Stitch markers

Stitch Glossary
Wrap 6 sts Insert RH needle between 6th and 7th sts on LH needle, wrap working yarn and pull up a loop on RS, place on LH needle. Pull working yarn gently to gather wrap sts, then knit loop st together with next st on needle.

Wrap 7 sts Insert RH needle between 7th and 8th sts on LH needle, wrap working yarn and pull up a loop on RS, place on LH needle. Pull working yarn gently to gather wrap sts, then knit loop st together with next st on needle.

Notes
Cowl is worked from the neck edge down.

Cowl
Cast on 160 sts. Join, taking care not to twist sts, and place marker for beg of rnd.

Rnd 1 *K2, p2; rep from * around.
Rep rnd 1 for k2, p2 rib for 9 rnds more.
Inc rnd *K5, M1; rep from * around—192 sts.
Knit 1 rnd.

BEG PATTERN STITCH
Rnd 1 [K1, yo, k4, SK2P, k4, yo] 16 times.
Rnd 2 and all even-numbered rnds Knit.
Rnd 3 [K2, yo, k3, SK2P, k3, yo, k1] 16 times.
Rnd 5 [K3, yo, wrap 7 sts, k1, SK2P, k2, yo, k2] 16 times.
Rnd 7 K2tog, [k4, yo, k1, yo, k4, SK2P] 15 times, k4, yo, k1, yo, k4, sl 1, remove marker, sl 1, pass first slipped st over last slipped st, sl st back to LH needle, replace marker.
Rnd 9 K2tog, [k3, yo, k3, yo, k3, SK2P] 15 times, k3, yo, k3, yo, k3, sl 1, remove marker, sl 1, pass first slipped st over last slipped st, sl st back to LH needle, replace marker.
Rnd 11 K2tog, [k2, yo, k5, yo, wrap 7 sts, k1, SK2P] 15 times, k2, yo, k5, yo, wrap 6 sts, k1, sl 1, remove marker, sl 1, pass first

Gauge
17 sts and 26 rnds to 4"/10cm over pat st using size 8 (5mm) needles.
Take time to check gauge.

Openwork Flair

slipped st over last slipped st, sl st back to LH needle, replace marker.

Rnd 12 (inc) *K3, M1; rep from * around—256 sts.

Rnd 13 [K1, yo, k2, p2, k2, SK2P, k2, p2, k2, yo] 16 times.

Rnd 15 [K2, yo, k1, p2, k2, SK2P, k2, p2, k1, yo, k1] 16 times.

Rnd 17 [K3, p2, yo, wrap 7 sts, k1, SK2P, k2, yo, p2, k2] 16 times.

Rnd 19 K2tog, [k2, p2, k2, yo, k1, yo, k2, p2, k2, SK2P] 15 times, k2, p2, k2, yo, k1, yo, k2, p2, k2, sl 1, remove marker, sl 1, pass first slipped st over last slipped st, sl

st back to LH needle, replace marker.

Rnd 21 K2tog, [k2, p2, k1, yo, k3, yo, k1, p2, k2, SK2P] 15 times, k2, p2, k1, yo, k3, yo, k1, p2, k2, sl 1, remove marker, sl 1, pass first slipped st over last slipped st, sl st back to LH needle, replace marker.

Rnd 23 K2tog, [k2, yo, p2, k5, p2, yo, wrap 7 sts, k1, SK2P] 15 times, k2, yo, p2, k5, p2, yo, wrap 6 sts, k1, sl 1, re-move marker, sl 1, pass first slipped st over last slipped st, sl st back to LH nee-dle, replace marker.

Rnd 24 (inc) *K4, M1; rep from * around—320 sts.

Rnd 25 [K1, yo, k2, p4, k2, SK2P, k2, p4, k2, yo] 16 times.

Rnd 27 [K2, yo, k1, p4, k2, SK2P, k2, p4, k1, yo, k1] 16 times.

Rnd 29 [K3, p4, yo, wrap 7 sts, k1, SK2P, k2, yo, p4, k2] 16 times.

Rnd 31 K2tog, [k2, p4, k2, yo, k1, yo, k2, p4, k2, SK2P] 15 times, k2, p4, k2, yo, k1, yo, k2, p4, k2, sl 1, remove marker, sl 1, pass first slipped st over last slipped st, sl st back to LH needle, replace marker.

Rnd 33 K2tog, [k2, p4, k1, yo, k3, yo, k1, p4, k2, SK2P] 15 times, k2, p4, k1, yo, k3, yo, k1, p4, k2, sl 1, remove marker, sl 1, pass first slipped st over last slipped st, sl st back to LH needle, replace marker.

Rnd 35 K2tog, [k2, yo, p4, k5, p4, yo, wrap 7 sts, k1, SK2P] 15 times, k2, yo, p4, k5, p4, yo, wrap 6 sts, k1, sl 1, re-move marker, sl 1, pass first slipped st over last slipped st, sl st back to LH nee-dle, replace marker.

Rnd 36 Knit.

Rnds 37–42 Rep rnds 25–30.

Knit 1 rnd.

Work in k2, p2 rib for 10 rnds. Knit 1 rnd. Bind off loosely. ∎

Wrap Party

Customize this reversible cable covered piece with your own shawl pin to turn a wrap into a cowl.

DESIGNED BY LINDA VOSS PLUMMER

Knitted Measurements
Width 10"/25.5cm
Length 31"/79cm

Materials
▪ 3 3½oz/100g hanks (each approx 164yd/150m) of Cascade Yarns *Cloud* (merino wool/baby alpaca) in #2133 faded denim (4)
▪ One pair size 9 (5.5mm) needles *or size to obtain gauge*
▪ Cable needle (cn)
▪ Stitch markers
▪ Shawl pin (optional)

Stitch Glossary
12-st rib RC Sl 6 sts to cn, hold to *back*, work 6 sts in rib, work 6 sts from cn in rib.
12-st rib LC Sl 6 sts to cn, hold to *front*, work 6 sts in rib, work 6 sts from cn in rib.
16-st rib RC Sl 8 sts to cn, hold to *back*, work 8 sts in rib, work 8 sts from cn in rib.
16-st rib LC Sl 8 sts to cn, hold to *front*, work 8 sts in rib, work 8 sts from cn in rib.

Note
Right and wrong sides are marked on chart; however, cowl is reversible.

Cowl
Cast on 85 sts.
Set-up row (WS) [K1, p1] 8 times, pm, *k1 (garter st column), [k2, p2] 3 times, pm; rep from * 3 times more, k1 (garter st column), [k1, p1] 8 times.
Work in rib and garter st columns as established, k the knit sts and garter st column sts, and p the purl sts, for 8 rows more, end with a WS row.

BEG CHART
Note Cables A and D have 16-row repeats (outlined in red), cables B and C have 12-row repeats (outlined in blue and green). Maintain k1, p1 rib as established over cables A and D, and k2, p2 rib as established over cables B and C. Cont to work garter st columns between each cable.
Row 1 (RS) Work cable A over 16 sts, [work cable B over 13 sts] twice, [work cable C over 13 sts] twice, work cable D over 17 sts.
Cont to work chart in this manner until piece measures 30"/76cm from beg, end with a row 18.
Work in rib and garter st columns as established for 8 rows. Bind off in rib. Wrap piece around shoulders and close with shawl pin if desired. ■

Gauge
34 sts and 22 rows to 4"/10cm over chart pat using size 9 (5.5mm) needles.
Take time to check gauge.

16

Wrap Party

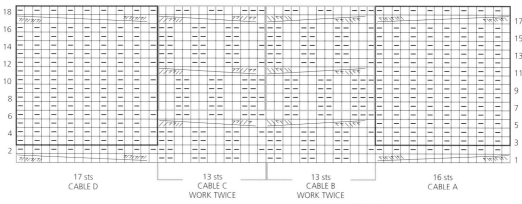

17 sts	13 sts	13 sts	16 sts
CABLE D	CABLE C	CABLE B	CABLE A
	WORK TWICE	WORK TWICE	

STITCH KEY

☐ k on RS, p on WS

— p on RS, k on WS

12-st rib RC

12-st rib LC

16-st rib I

16-st rib I

Intarsia Ribs

Geometric blocks of color formed with intarsia
liven up a simple ribbed shape.

DESIGNED BY AUDREY DRYSDALE

Knitted Measurements
Circumference 26"/66cm
Length 9½"/24cm

Materials
■ 1 3½oz/100g hanks (each approx
164yd/150m) of Cascade Yarns *Cloud*
(merino wool/baby alpaca) each in
#2130 loganberry (A), #2131 anemone
(B), and #2115 raspberry (C) (4)
■ Size 8 (5mm) circular needle,
24"/60cm long, *or size to obtain gauge*
■ Stitch marker

Stitch Glossary
K1b Knit 1 in row below.

Rib Pattern
(over an odd number of sts)
Row 1 (RS) K1, *k1b, p1; rep from * to
last 2 sts, k1b, k1.

Row 2 (WS) Knit.
Rep rows 1 and 2 for rib pat.

Note
When changing colors, twist yarns on
WS to prevent holes in work. If color
change falls on a purl stitch in rib pat,
work a knit stitch instead, then cont in
pat.

Cowl
With A, cast on 115 sts. Purl 1 row. Do
not join, work back and forth in rows.

BEG CHART AND RIB PATTERN
Row 1 (RS) With A, k1, *k1b, p1; rep
from * to last 2 sts, k1b, k1.
Row 2 (WS) With A, knit.
Row 3 With A, k1, *k1b, p1; rep from *
to last 2 sts, with B, k1b, k1.
Row 4 With B, k2, with A, k to end.
Cont to work chart and rib pat in this
way through row 84 of chart. Bind off in
chart pat.

Finishing
Sew back seam. ■

Gauge
16 sts and 32 rows to 4"/10cm over rib pattern using size 8 (5mm) needle.
Take time to check gauge.

Intarsia Ribs

17

COLOR KEY

▨ Loganberry (A)

■ Anemone (B)

▨ Raspberry (C)

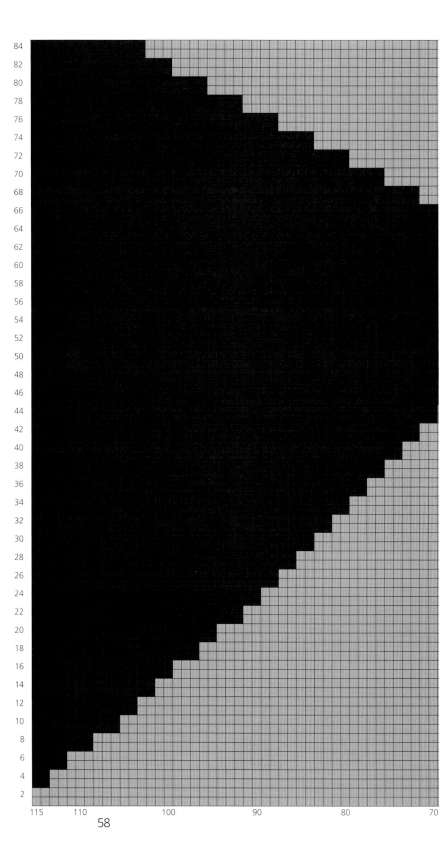

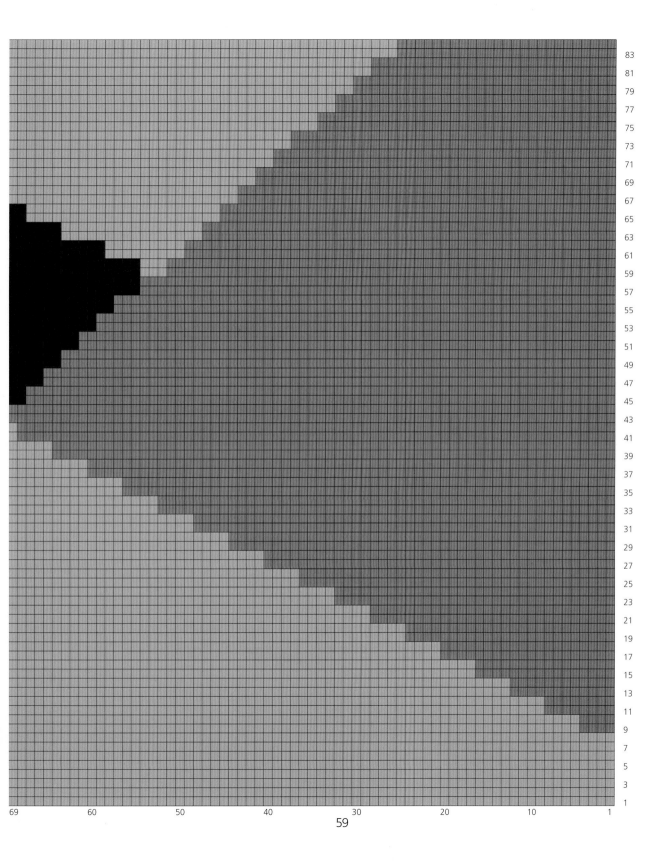

18

Slip Stitch Stripes

Neutral stripes are broken by slipped stitches in a softly pretty piece that enhances any outfit.

DESIGNED BY GRACE AKHREM

Knitted Measurements
Circumference 23"/58.5cm
Length 9"/23cm

Materials
■ 1 3½oz/100g hank (each approx
164yd/150m) of Cascade Yarns
Eco Cloud (merino wool/baby alpaca)
each in #1810 charcoal (A) and #1809
dove gray (B)
■ Size 9 (5.5mm) circular needle,
16"/40cm long, *or size to obtain gauge*
■ Stitch marker

Notes
Carry color not in use loosely up inside
of work. Slip sts purlwise with yarn in
back.

Cowl
With A, cast on 92 sts. Join, taking care
not to twist sts, and place marker for
beg of rnd.
[Purl 1 rnd, knit 1 rnd] 3 times.

BEG PATTERN STITCH
Rnd 1 With A, knit.
Rnds 2, 3, and 4 With B, *k3, sl 1 wyib;
rep from * around.
Rnd 5 With A, knit.
Rnd 6 With B, knit.
Rnds 7, 8, and 9 With A, *k1, sl 1 wyib,
k2; rep from * around.
Rnd 10 with B, knit.
Rep rnds 1–10 three times more, then
rep rnds 1–5 once more.

With A, [knit 1 rnd, purl 1 rnd] 3 times.
Bind off loosely.

Finishing
Block lightly to measurements.■

Gauge
16 sts and 26 rnds to 4"/10cm over pattern st using size 9 (5.5mm) needle.
Take time to check gauge.

Chevron Chic

A bright color pops with modern black and grey in a subtle, sophisticated design of chevron stripes.

DESIGNED BY DEBBIE O'NEILL

Knitted Measurements
Circumference 23"/58.5cm
Length 6½"/15cm

Materials
■ 1 3½oz/100g hank (each approx 197yd/180m) of Cascade Yarns *Highland Duo* (baby alpaca/merino wool) each in #2303 grey (A), #2302 black (B), and #2300 ruby (C) (4)
■ One pair size 6 (4mm) needles *or size to obtain gauge*
■ One spare size 6 (4mm) needle for 3-needle bind-off
■ Size G/6 (4mm) crochet hook and scrap yarn for provisional cast-on

Provisional Cast-On
Using scrap yarn and crochet hook, chain the number of sts to cast on, plus a few extra. Cut a tail and pull the tail through the last chain. With knitting needle and yarn, pick up and knit the stated number of sts through the "purl bumps" on the back of the chain. To remove scrap chain, when instructed, pull out the tail from the last crochet st. Gen-

tly and slowly pull on the tail to unravel the crochet sts, carefully placing each released knit st on a needle.

3-Needle Bind-Off
1) Hold right sides of pieces together on 2 needles. Insert 3rd needle knitwise into first st of each needle and wrap yarn knitwise.
2) Knit these 2 sts together and slip

them off the needles. *Knit the next 2 sts together in the same manner.
3) Slip first st on 3rd needle over 2nd st and off needle. Rep from * in step 2 across row until all sts are bound off.

Chevron Pattern
(multiple of 12 sts plus 3)
Row 1 (RS) K1, k2tog, *k4, (k1, yo, k1) in the next stitch, k4, S2KP; rep from *, end last rep ssk, k1.
Row 2 Purl.
Rep rows 1 and 2 for chevron pat.

Cowl
With A, cast on 39 sts using provisional cast-on. Purl 1 row on WS.
Working in chevron pat, work stripe pattern as foll:
14 rows A, 6 rows B, 4 rows A, 2 rows C, 12 rows A, 8 rows B, 4 rows A, 2 rows B, 10 rows A, 2 rows C, 22 rows A, 4 rows B, 2 rows A, 2 rows C, 10 rows A, 6 rows B, 8 rows A, 2 rows B, 4 rows A. Carefully remove provisional cast-on and place sts on needle. Join first row to last row using 3-needle bind-off. Block lightly to measurements. ■

Gauge
24 sts and 22 rows to 4"/10cm over chevron pat using size 6 (4mm) needles.
Take time to check gauge.

Sea of Scallops

Scallops created by short rows in alternating colors create a dimension in a sweet shoulder warmer.

DESIGNED BY AMANDA BLAIR BROWN

Knitted Measurements
Circumference 36"/91.5cm
Length 10"/25.5cm

Materials
- 2 3½oz/100g hanks (each approx 164yd/150m) of Cascade Yarns *Cloud* (merino wool/baby alpaca) each in #2114 plum (A) and #2113 lilac (B) (4)
- Size 9 (5.5mm) circular needle, 32"/80cm long, *or size to obtain gauge*
- Stitch markers

Short Row Wrap & Turn (w&t)
on RS row (on WS row)
1) Wyib (wyif), sl next st purlwise.
2) Move yarn between the needles to the front (back).
3) Sl the same st back to LH needle. Turn work. One st is wrapped.

4) When working the wrapped st, insert RH needle under the wrap and work it tog with the corresponding st on needle.

Cowl
With A, cast on 144 sts. Join, taking care not to twist sts, and place marker for beg of rnd. Purl 1 rnd.

BEG PATTERN STITCH
Rnd 1 With A, *k11, w&t, p10, w&t, k9, w&t, p8, w&t, k7, w&t, p6, w&t, k5, w&t, p4, w&t, k3, w&t, p2, w&t, k7, picking up wraps; rep from * around.
Rnd 2 With A, knit, picking up rem wraps. Break A, leaving long tail.
Rnd 3 Sl 6 sts purlwise, place 2nd marker for alternate beg of rnd. With B, *k11, w&t, p10, w&t, k9, w&t, p8, w&t, k7, w&t, p6, w&t, k5, w&t, p4, w&t, k3, w&t, p2, w&t, k7, picking up wraps; rep from * around, ending at alternate marker.
Rnd 4 With B, knit, picking up rem wraps, ending at alternate marker. Break B, leaving long tail. Remove alternate marker, slip last 6 sts on RH needle back to LH needle, rnd begins at original marker.
Rep rnds 1–4 three times more, then work rnd 1 once more. With A, purl 1 rnd. Bind off knitwise.

Finishing
Block lightly to measurements. ■

Gauge
16 sts and 24 rnds to 4"/10cm over St st using size 9 (5.5mm) needle.
Take time to check gauge.

Check Mate

A simple miniature checkerboard pattern covers a modern
design that works with every style.

DESIGNED BY SHEILA JOYNES

Knitted Measurements
Circumference 25"/63.5cm
Length 11"/28cm

Materials
- 1 3½oz/100g hank (each approx
197yd/180m) of Cascade Yarns *Highland
Duo* (baby alpaca/merino wool) each in
#2316 dusty teal (A) and #2324 dark
blue (B) (**4**)
- Size 10 (6mm) circular needle,
16"/40cm long, *or size to obtain gauge*
- Stitch marker

Note
When changing colors, twist yarns on
WS to prevent holes in work.

Rnd 4 *P2 B, p2 A; rep from * around.
Rep rnds 1–4 for pattern stitch until
piece measures 11"/28cm from beg.
With B, bind off. Block lightly to
measurements. ■

Cowl
With B, cast on 148 sts. Join, taking care
not to twist sts, and place marker for
beg of rnd.
Rnd 1 *K2 A, k2 B; rep from * around.
Rnd 2 *P2 A, p2 B; rep from * around.
Rnd 3 *K2 B, k2 A; rep from * around.

Gauge
24 sts and 26 rnds to 4"/10cm over pat st using size 10 (6mm) needle.
Take time to check gauge.

Tied in Knots

An easy-to-knit ribbed strip becomes a unique style statement tied in a chunky knot before the ends are grafted.

DESIGNED BY ALICE TANG

■■□▷

Knitted Measurements
Circumference (tied) 22"/56cm
Length 6¾"/17cm

Materials
▥ 1 3½oz/100g hank (each approx 197yd/180m) of Cascade Yarns *Eco Duo* (baby alpaca/merino wool) in #1707 latte (**4**)
▥ One pair size 8 (5mm) needles, *or size to obtain gauge*
▥ Scrap yarn and crochet hook for provisional cast-on

Provisional Cast-On
Using scrap yarn and crochet hook, chain the number of sts to cast on, plus a few extra. Cut a tail and pull the tail through the last chain. With knitting needle and yarn, pick up and knit the stated number of sts through the "purl bumps" on the back of the chain. To remove scrap chain, when instructed, pull out the tail from the last crochet st. Gently and slowly pull on the tail to unravel the crochet sts, carefully placing each released knit st on a needle.

3-Needle Bind-Off
1) Hold right sides of pieces together on 2 needles. Insert 3rd needle knitwise into first st of each needle and wrap yarn knitwise.
2) Knit these 2 sts together and slip them off the needles. *Knit the next 2 sts together in the same manner.
3) Slip first st on 3rd needle over 2nd st and off needle. Rep from * in step 2 across row until all sts are bound off.

Cowl
Cast-on 44 sts using provisional cast-on method.
Row 1 *K1, p1; rep from * to end.
Rep row 1 for k1, p1 rib until hank is almost complete, leaving a tail approx 40"/101.5cm long.
Tie an overhand knot in work. Carefully remove provisional cast-on and join to final row of work using 3-needle bind-off. Adjust knot so join is hidden behind knot.■

Gauge
26 sts and 22 rows to 4"/10cm over k1, p1 rib using size 8 (5mm) needles.
Take time to check gauge.

23

Sweet & Simple

A quick and easy knit with Stockinette stitch and garter ridges is elevated to elegance in a rich tonal colorway.

DESIGNED BY CHARLES GANDY

■■□□

Knitted Measurements
Circumference 23½"/59.5cm
Length 12"/30.5cm

Materials
▨ 2 3½oz/100g hanks (each approx 197yd/180m) of Cascade Yarns *Color Duo* (baby alpaca/merino wool) in #206 treetop (**4**)
▨ Size 8 (5mm) circular needle, 16"/40cm long, *or size to obtain gauge*
▨ Stitch marker

measures 8"/20.5cm from last purl rnd.
[Purl 3 rnds, knit 5 rnds] twice, purl 3 rnds.
Bind off. Block lightly.■

Cowl
Cast on 112 sts. Join, taking care not to twist sts, and place marker for beg of rnd.
[Purl 3 rnds, knit 5 rnds] twice, purl 3 rnds.
Work in St st (k every rnd) until piece

Gauge
19 sts and 24 rnds to 4"/10cm over St st using size 8 (5mm) needles.
Take time to check gauge.

Travel Time

Traveling cables framed by moss stitch edges make a beautiful blend of texture and movement.

DESIGNED BY FAINA GOBERSTEIN

Knitted Measurements
Circumference approx 35"/89cm
Length 9"/23cm

Materials
■ 2 3½oz/100g hanks (each approx 164yd/150m) of Cascade Yarns *Cloud* (merino wool/baby alpaca) in #2135 turquoise
■ One pair size 9 (5.5mm) needles *or size to obtain gauge*
■ Cable needle (cn)

Stitch Glossary
4-st LC Sl 2 to cn and hold to *front*, k2, k2 from cn.

Traveling Cable Pattern
(multiple of 6 sts plus 4)
Row 1 (RS) K2, *k2, p2, k2; rep from * to last 2 sts, k2.
Row 2 P2, *p2, k2, p2; rep from * to last 2 sts, p2.

Row 3 Rep row 1.
Row 4 Rep row 2.
Row 5 *4-st LC, p2; rep from * to last 4 sts, 4-st LC.
Row 6 Rep row 2.
Row 7 Rep row 1.
Row 8 Rep row 2.

Row 9 K1, p1, *p1, k4, p1; rep from * to last 2 sts, p1, k1.
Row 10 P1, k1, *k1, p4, k1; rep from * to last 2 sts, k1, p1.
Row 11 Rep row 9.
Row 12 Rep row 10.
Row 13 K1, p1, *p1, 4-st LC, p1; rep from * to last 2 sts, p1, k1.
Row 14 Rep row 10.
Row 15 Rep row 9.
Row 16 Rep row 10.
Rep rows 1–16 for traveling cable pat.

Note
Traveling cable pat can be worked from text *or* chart.

Cowl
Cast on 50 sts.
Rows 1 and 3 (RS) Sl 1, *k1, p1; rep from * to last st, k1.
Row 2 Sl 1, *p1, k1; rep from * to last st, p1.

BEGIN TRAVELING CABLE PAT
Row 1 (RS) Sl 1, [k1, p1] twice, work row 1 of traveling cable pat over 40 sts, [k1, p1] twice, k1.

Gauge
23 sts and 28 rows to 4"/10cm over traveling cable pat using size 9 (5.5mm) needles.
Take time to check gauge.

Travel Time

Cont to work pat in this manner, keeping first and last 5 sts in seed st and center 40 sts in traveling cable pat as established, until piece measures approx 34"/86.5cm from beg, end with a cable pat row 7.
Work 3 rows in seed st over all sts for border.
Bind off in pat.

Finishing
Sew bound-off and cast-on edges tog to form cowl.■

TRAVELING RIB CHART

6-st rep

STITCH KEY

☐ k on RS, p on WS

☐ p on RS, k on WS

⬚ 4-st LC

Bobble Flowers

Front ties add versatility to a beautiful botanical design, with bobbles and cables forming leaves and flowers.

DESIGNED BY ANNE JONES

◼◼◼▢

Knitted Measurements
Length (excluding ties) 34"/86.5cm
Width 6½"/16.5cm

Materials
▪ 2 3½oz/100g hanks (each approx 197yd/180m) of Cascade Yarns *Eco Highland Duo* (baby alpaca/merino wool) in #2204 ecru (**4**)
▪ One pair size 7 (4.5mm) needles *or size to obtain gauge*
▪ Cable needle (cn)
▪ Stitch markers

Stitch Glossary
2-st RC (RS) Sl 1 st to cn, hold to *back*, k1, k1 from cn.
2-st RC (WS) Sl 1 st to cn, hold to *back*, p1, p1 from cn.
2-st LC (RS) Sl 1 st to cn, hold to *front*, k1, k1 from cn.
2-st LC (WS) Sl 1 st to cn, hold to *front*, p1, p1 from cn.
2-st RPC (RS) Sl 1 st to cn, hold to *back*, k1, p1 from cn.
2-st RPC (WS) Sl 1 st to cn, hold to *back*, p1, k1 from cn.
2-st LPC (RS) Sl 1 st to cn, hold to *front*, k1, p1 from cn.
2-st LPC (WS) Sl 1 st to cn, hold to *front*, p1, k1 from cn.
MB (make bobble) K into the fbfbf of next st, [sl 5 sts back to LH needle, k5] twice, sl 5 sts back to LH needle, k2tog tbl, k1, k2tog, sl 3 sts back to LH needle with yarn in front, running yarn under bobble to cinch, p3tog.

Cowl
Cast on 7 sts.
Row 1 [K1, p1] 3 times, k1.
Rep row 1 for seed stitch until tie measures 14"/35.5cm.

BEG EDGING
Next row (RS) [K1, p1] 3 times, k1, cast on 32 sts—39 sts.
Edging row (WS) *K1, p1; rep from *

Gauge
25 sts and 30 rows to 4"/10cm over chart using size 7 (4.5mm) needles.
Take time to check gauge.

25 Bobble Flowers

to last st, k1.
Rep edging row for 8 rows more.
BEG CHART

Row 1 (RS) [K1, p1] 3 times, k1, pm, work chart over 25 sts, pm, [k1, p1] 3 times, k1. Working 7 sts each side in seed stitch as established, cont to work chart in this manner until 40 rows of chart have been worked 6 times.

Edging row (RS) *K1, p1; rep from * to last st, k1.
Rep edging row for 8 rows more.

Next row (WS) Bind off 32 sts in pat, work 7 sts as established.
Cont in seed st over 7 sts until tie measures 14"/35.5cm. Bind off in pat.

Finishing
Block lightly to measurements. ∎

STITCH KEY

☐	p on RS, k on WS
▨	k on RS, p on WS
ℚ	k1tbl on RS, p1tbl on WS
●	make bobble (MB)
⧅	2-st RC (RS)
⧅	2-st RC (WS)
⧄	2-st LC (RS)
⧄	2-st LC (WS)
⧅	2-st RPC (RS)
⧅	2-st RPC (WS)
⧄	2-st LPC (RS)
⧄	2-st LPC (WS)

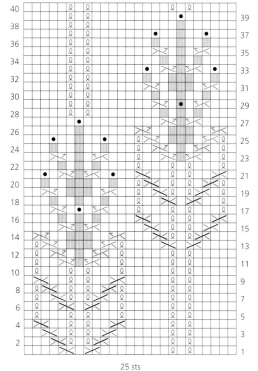

25 sts

26

Ribs with a Twist

A simple ribbed loop catches the eye when a twisted traveling cable is added to the picture.

DESIGNED BY CHERYL LAVENHAR

Knitted Measurements
Circumference 44"/111.5cm
Width (slightly stretched) 6"/15cm

Materials
- 2 3½oz/100g hanks (each approx 164yd/150m) of Cascade Yarns *Cloud* (merino wool/baby alpaca) in #2107 geranium (4)
- One pair size 10 (6mm) needles *or size to obtain gauge*
- Stitch markers
- Cable needle (cn)

Stitch Glossary
8-st RC Sl 4 sts to cn, hold to *back*, work 4 sts in rib pat, work 4 sts from cn in rib pat.
8-st LC Sl 4 sts to cn, hold to *front*, work 4 sts in rib pat, work 4 sts from cn in rib pat.

Cowl
Cast on 40 sts.
Row 1 (RS) *K2, p2; rep from * to end.
Row 2 (WS) K the knit sts and p the purl sts.
Rep rows 1 and 2 once more for k2, p2 rib.
Row 5 8-st LC, work in rib to end.

Work 7 rows in k2, p2 rib as established. Rep last 8 rows once more.
Row 21 Work 4 sts in rib, place marker (pm), 8-st LC, work in rib to end.
Work 7 rows in rib. Rep last 8 rows once more, slipping marker.
Next row Work in rib to marker, remove marker, work 4 sts in rib, pm, 8-st LC, work in rib to end. Work 7 rows in rib.
Next row Work in rib to marker, 8-st LC, work in rib to end. Work 7 rows in rib.
Rep last 16 rows 6 times more, therefore shifting 8-st LC over 4 sts to the left every 16 rows and the last cable will be worked over last 8 sts of last rep.
Next row Work in rib to 4 sts before marker, place new marker, 8-st RC (removing original marker), work in rib to end. Work 7 rows in rib.
Next row Work in rib to marker, sl marker, 8-st RC, work in rib to end. Work 7 rows in rib.
Rep last 16 rows 6 times more, therefore shifting 8-st LC over 4 sts to the left every 16 rows and the last cable will be worked over sts 5–12. Work 5 rows in k2, p2 rib after the final cable row.
Bind off in rib. Sew bound-off edge to cast-on edge.■

Gauge
24 sts and 24 rows to 4"/10cm over k2, p2 rib, slightly stretched, using size 10 (6mm) needles.
Take time to check gauge.

Ruffled Heathers

Soft ruffles along both edges are softened even further
by a pair of neutral colorways.

DESIGNED BY BETH WHITESIDE

Knitted Measurements
Circumference 44"/111.5cm
Width 6"/15cm

Materials
▓ 1 3½oz/100g hank (each approx
197yd/180m) of Cascade Yarns *Eco Duo*
(baby alpaca/merino wool) in #1709
burlywood (4)
▓ 1 3½oz/100g hank (each approx
197yd/180m) of Cascade Yarns *Eco
Highland Duo* (baby alpaca/merino wool)
in #2203 café au lait (B) (4)
▓ One each sizes 4 and 9 (3.5 and
5.5mm) circular needles, 32"/80cm long,
or size to obtain gauge
▓ Size G/6 (4mm) crochet hook and
scrap yarn for provisional cast-on
▓ Stitch marker

Note
Cowl is worked in the round from the
center out. After the first side is worked,
the second side is picked up from the
provisional cast-on and worked.

COWL
With smaller needle and A, cast on
264 sts using provisional cast-on
method. Join and place marker (pm)
for beg of rnd. **Beg with a purl rnd,
work in garter st (purl 1 rnd, knit 1
rnd) for 11 rnds. Change to larger
needle.

Next rnd (dec) [K3, k2tog, k4, ssk] 24
times—216 sts.

BEG RUFFLE PATTERN
Rnds 1 and 2 *K1, p7, rep from *
around.
Rnd 3 *Yo, k1, yo, p7; rep from *
around—270 sts.
Rnd 4 *K1 tbl, k1, k1 tbl, p7; rep from *
around.
Rnd 5 *Yo, k3, yo, p7; rep from *
around—324 sts.
Rnd 6 *K1 tbl, k3, k1 tbl, p7; rep from *
around.
Cont increasing every other round as
established 3 times more—486 sts.
Rnd 12 *K1 tbl, k9, k1 tbl, p7; rep from
* around.
Bind off loosely in pat.

Carefully remove provisional cast-on and
place sts on smaller needle. With B,
work as for first side from **.
Block gently.▄

Gauge
24 sts and 48 rnds to 4"/10cm over garter st using size 4 (3.5mm) needle.
Take time to check gauge.

Bold Shoulders

Bobbles spice up bands of dropped stitches and garter stitch, while ribs hug the neck and shoulders.

DESIGNED BY DEBORAH HELMKE

Knitted Measurements
Circumference at lower edge
26"/66cm
Depth 13"/33cm

Materials
▪ 2 3½oz/100g hanks (each approx 197yd/180m) of Cascade Yarns *Highland Duo* (baby alpaca/merino wool) in #2316 dusty teal (**4**)
▪ One each sizes 7 and 8 (4.5 and 5mm) circular needles, 24"/60cm long, *or size to obtain gauge*
▪ Stitch marker

Stitch Glossary
MB (make bobble) (K1, yo, k1, yo, k1) into next st, turn, p5, turn, k5, turn, p2tog, p1, p2tog, turn, S2KP.

Cowl
With smaller needle, cast on 130 sts. Do *not* join.

Row 1 (RS) K2, *p2, k2; rep from * to end.
Row 2 K the knit sts and p the purl sts.
Rep row 2 for k2, p2 rib for 2"/5cm, end with a WS row.
Next row (RS) K1, [k2tog, k4] 21 times, k2tog, k1—108 sts.
Join and place marker (pm) for beg of rnd. Change to larger needle.

Knit 4 rnds.
Change to smaller needle and beg texture sequence.
Rnd 1 *K1, wrapping yarn twice; rep from * around.
Rnd 2 Purl, dropping extra wraps.
[K 1 rnd, p 1 rnd] twice, k 1 rnd.
Change to larger needle.
Rnds 8 and 9 Knit.
Rnd 10 *MB, k5; rep from * around.
Knit 2 rnds.
Rnd 13 *K3, MB, k2; rep from * around.
Knit 2 rnds.
Rnd 16 *MB, k5; rep from * around.
Knit 2 rnds.
Change to smaller needle.
Rnd 19 Knit.
[P 1 rnd, k 1 rnd] twice, p 1 rnd.
Rnd 25 *K1, wrapping yarn twice; rep from * around.
Change to larger needle.
Rnd 26 Knit, dropping extra wraps.
Knit 3 rnds.
Change to smaller needle.
Next rnd *K2, p2; rep from * around.
Rep last rnd for k2, p2 rib for 6"/15cm.
Bind off in rib.■

Gauges
20 sts and 24 rows/rnds to 4"/10cm over k2, p2 rib using size 7 (4.5mm) needle.
16 sts and 24 rnds to 4"10cm over St st using size 8 (5mm) needle.
Take time to check gauges.

Lattice Bliss

Loads of crisscrossed cables cover a long loop
that can be wrapped twice for double the warmth.

DESIGNED BY SUSIE ALLEN

Knitted Measurements
Circumference 48"/123cm
Length 7"/18cm

Materials
■ 2 3½oz/100g hanks (each approx
197yd/180m) of Cascade Yarns *Eco Duo*
(baby alpaca/merino wool) in #1708
hazelnut (4)
■ One pair size 10 (6mm) needles
or size to obtain gauge
■ One spare size 10 (6mm) needle for
3-needle bind-off
■ Size J/10 (6mm) crochet hook and
scrap yarn for provisional cast-on
■ Cable needle (cn)
■ Stitch marker

Provisional Cast-On
Using scrap yarn and crochet hook, chain
the number of sts to cast on, plus a few
extra. Cut a tail and pull the tail through
the last chain. With knitting needle and
yarn, pick up and knit the stated number
of sts through the "purl bumps" on the
back of the chain. To remove scrap chain,
when instructed, pull out the tail from the

last crochet st. Gently and slowly pull on
the tail to unravel the crochet sts, carefully
placing each released knit st on a needle.

3-Needle Bind-Off
1) Hold right sides of pieces together on 2
needles. Insert 3rd needle knitwise into first
st of each needle and wrap yarn knitwise.
2) Knit these 2 sts together and slip
them off the needles. *Knit the next 2
sts together in the same manner.
3) Slip first st on 3rd needle over 2nd st
and off needle. Rep from * in step 2
across row until all sts are bound off.

Stitch Glossary
4-st RC Sl 2 sts to cn, hold to *back*, k2,
k2 from cn.

4-st LC Sl 2 sts to cn, hold to *front*, k2,
k2 from cn.
4-st RPC Sl 2 sts to cn, hold to *back*, k2,
p2 from cn.
4-st LPC Sl 2 sts to cn, hold to *front*, p2,
k2 from cn.

Cowl
Cast on 50 sts using provisional cast-on.
Row 1 (RS) P3, 4-st RC, *p4, 4-st RC;
rep from * to last 3 sts, p3.
Row 2 (WS) K3, p4, *k4, p4; rep from *
to last 3 sts, k3.
Row 3 P1, *4-st RPC, 4-st LPC; rep from
* to last st, p1.
Row 4 K1, p2, k4, *p4, k4; rep from *
to last 3 sts, p2, k1.
Row 5 P1, k2, p4, *4-st RC, p4; rep
from * to last 3 sts, k2, p1.
Row 6 Rep row 4.
Row 7 P1, *4-st LPC, 4-st RPC; rep from
* to last st, p1.
Row 8 Rep row 2.
Rep rows 1–8 until piece measures approx 48"/123cm.
Carefully remove provisional cast-on and
place sts on needle. Join last row to cast-on row with 3-needle bind-off. ■

Gauge
24 sts and 25 rows to 4"/10cm over pat st using size 10 (6mm) needles.
Take time to check gauge.

30

In the Loop

Elongated loop stitches form mini eyelets in a pretty allover pattern that evokes a field of flowers.

DESIGNED BY FAINA GOBERSTEIN

Knitted Measurements
Circumference 19"/48cm
Length 7½"/19cm

Materials
▦ 1 3½oz/100g hank (each approx 197yd/180m) of Cascade Yarns *Highland Duo* (baby alpaca/merino wool) in #2322 loden (▣)
▦ Size 8 (5mm) circular needle, 16"/40cm long, *or size to obtain gauge*
▦ Stitch marker

Note
Stitch count changes from round to round in mini eyelets pattern.

Stitch Glossary
EL (elongated loop) With yarn in back of work, insert RH needle from front to back 2 rows below through opening made by k2tog and ssk, draw up a loop and place on RH needle.

Mini Eyelets Pattern
(multiple of 8 sts)
Rnd 1 *K4, k2tog, ssk; rep from * around.
Rnd 2 and all even-numbered rnds Knit.
Rnd 3 *K4, EL, k2, EL; rep from * around.
Rnd 5 *K2tog, ssk, k4; rep from * around.
Rnd 7 *EL, k2, EL, k4; rep from * around.
Rnd 8 Knit.
Rep rnds 1–8 for mini eyelets pat.

Cowl
Cast on 96 sts. Join, taking care not to twist sts, and place marker for beg of rnd. Knit 1 rnd, purl 1 rnd, knit 1 rnd. Work rnds 1–8 of mini eyelet pattern 6 times, then work rnds 1–4 once more. Purl 1 rnd, knit 1 rnd. Bind off.

Finishing
Block lightly. ▪

Gauge
20 sts and 31 rnds to 4"/10cm over mini eyelets pat using size 8 (5mm) needles.
Take time to check gauge.

Bounty of Bobbles

A popcorn pattern of allover bobbles on an oversized loop is plush and playful.

DESIGNED BY SHEILA JOYNES

Knitted Measurements
Circumference, measured over bobble pat 51¼"/130cm
Length 6"/15cm

Materials
▪ 2 3½oz/100g hanks (each approx 197yd/180m) of Cascade Yarns *Highland Duo* (baby alpaca/merino wool) in #2321 golden (4)
▪ Size 10 (6mm) circular needle, 24"/60cm long, *or size to obtain gauge*
▪ Stitch marker

Stitch Glossary
MB (make bobble) [Kfb] 3 times in same st—6 sts; turn, p6; turn, k6; turn, [p2tog] 3 times; turn, SK2P.

Bobble Pattern
(multiple of 6 sts)
Rnd 1 *K1, MB, k1, p3; rep from * around.
Rnds 2 and 3 Knit.
Rnd 4 *P3, k1, MB, k1; rep from * around.
Rnds 5 and 6 Knit.
Rep rnds 1–6 for bobble pat.

Cowl
Cast on 192 sts. Join, taking care not to twist sts, and place marker for beg of rnd. Work 6 rnds in garter st (k 1 rnd, p 1 rnd).

BEGIN BOBBLE PAT
Work rnds 1–6 of bobble pat 4 times, then rep rnds 1 and 2 once more. Beg with a p rnd, work 5 rnds garter st. Bind off loosely. ▪

Gauge
15 sts and 23 rnds to 4"/10cm over bobble pat using size 10 (6mm) needle.
Take time to check gauge.

Granny Square Glam

A little crochet goes a long way in an oversized ring of granny squares with a knitted rib edging.

DESIGNED BY STACEY GERBMAN

■■■▢

Knitted Measurements
Circumference 48"/122cm
Length 11½"/29cm

Materials
- 2 3½oz/100g hanks (each approx 164yd/150m) of Cascade Yarns *Eco Cloud* (merino wool/baby alpaca) in #1810 charcoal (A) (4)
- 1 hank each in #1801 cream (B), #1807 otter (C), and #1803 fawn (D)
- Size K/10.5 (6.5mm) crochet hook
- Size 9 (5.5mm) circular needle, 32"/80cm long, *or size to obtain gauge*
- Stitch marker

Note
Cowl is constructed of granny squares sewn into a ring. Ribbed edge is picked up and worked after ring is completed.

Granny Square (make 6)
With B, ch 4. Join ch with a sl st, forming a ring.

Rnd 1 (RS) Ch 3 (counts as 1 dc), work 2 dc in ring, ch 2, [work 3 dc in ring, ch 2] 3 times, join with a sl st in top of beg ch-3. Fasten off B.
Rnd 2 Join C with a sl st in any corner ch-2 sp. Ch 3, work 2 dc in same ch-2 sp, ch 2, work 3 dc in same ch-2 sp, ch 2, [(3 dc, ch 2, 3 dc) in next ch-2 sp, ch 2] 3 times, join with a sl st in top of beg ch-3.
Rnd 3 With C, ch 5, (3 dc, ch 2, 3 dc) in next ch-2 sp, [ch 2, 3 dc in next ch-2 sp, ch 2, (3 dc, ch 2, 3 dc) in next ch-2 sp] 3 times, ch 2, 2 dc in next ch-2 sp, join with a sl st in 3rd st of beg ch-5. Fasten off C.
Rnd 4 Join D with a sl st in any corner ch-2 sp. Ch 3, work 2 dc in same ch-2 sp, ch 2, work 3 dc in same ch-2 sp, ch 2, *[work 3 dc in next ch-2 sp, ch 2] twice, (3 dc, ch 2, 3 dc in next ch-2 sp), ch 2; rep from * twice more, [work 3 dc in next ch-2 sp, ch 2] twice, join with a sl st in top of beg ch-3. Fasten off D.
Rnd 5 Join A with a sl st in any corner ch-2 sp. Ch 3, work 2 dc in same ch-2 sp, ch 2, work 3 dc in same ch-2 sp, ch 2, *[work 3 dc in next ch-2 sp, ch 2] 3 times, (3 dc, ch 2, 3 dc in next ch-2 sp), ch 2; rep from * twice more, [work 3 dc in next ch-2 sp, ch 2] 3 times, join with a sl st in top of beg ch-3.
Rnd 6 With A, ch 5, (3 dc, ch 2, 3 dc) in next ch-3 sp, ch 2, *[work 3 dc in next ch-2 sp, ch 2] 4 times, (3 dc, ch 2, 3 dc

Gauge
1 granny square equals 8"/20.5cm square using size K/10.5 (6.5mm) hook.
Take time to check gauge.

32

Granny Square Glam

in next ch-2 sp), ch 2; rep from * twice more, [work 3 dc in next ch-2 sp, ch 2] 3 times, 2 dc in next ch-2 sp, join with a sl st in 3rd st of beg ch-5. Fasten off A.

Cowl
With WS together and A, seam squares in a strip using sl st. Join edges of first and last squares to form cowl.

EDGING
With RS facing, circular needle and A, pick up and k 188 sts along edge of joined cowl, working under both loops of dc at edge. Join and place marker for beg of rnd.
Rnd 1 With A, *k2, p2; rep from * around.
Rep rnd 1 for k2, p2 rib, working in stripe sequence as foll: 3 additional rnds A, 2 rnds D, 2 rnds C, 2 rnds B.
With B, bind off loosely in rib.
Work edging in same way around opposite edge. ■

Ribbon Waves

A matching zigzag ribbon is woven through dropped stitches to create sophisticated, satiny stripes.

DESIGNED BY WEI WILKINS

Knitted Measurements
Circumference 28"/71cm
Length 11½"/29cm

Materials
■ 2 3½oz/100g hanks (each approx 197yd/180m) of Cascade Yarns *Highland Duo* (baby alpaca/merino wool) in #2314 meadow (**4**)

■ One pair size 6 (4mm) needles *or size to obtain gauge*

■ One additional size 6 (4mm) needle for 3-needle bind-off

■ Size G/6 (4mm) crochet hook and scrap yarn for provisional cast-on

■ 3⅓yd/3m of silky zigzag ribbon, ½"/1cm wide

■ Stitch markers

■ Stitch holders

■ Sewing needle and matching thread

Provisional Cast-On
Using scrap yarn and crochet hook, chain the number of sts to cast on, plus a few extra. Cut a tail and pull the tail through the last chain. With knitting needle and yarn, pick up and knit the stated number of sts through the "purl bumps" on the back of the chain. To remove scrap chain, when instructed, pull out the tail from the last crochet st. Gently and slowly pull on the tail to unravel the crochet sts, carefully placing each released knit st on a needle.

3-Needle Bind-Off
1) Hold right sides of pieces together on 2 needles. Insert 3rd needle knitwise into first st of each needle and wrap yarn knitwise.
2) Knit these 2 sts together and slip them off the needles. *Knit the next 2 sts together in the same manner.
3) Slip first st on 3rd needle over 2nd st and off needle. Rep from * in step 2 across row until all sts are bound off.

Cowl
Cast on 76 sts using provisional cast-on.
Row 1 *K1, p1; rep from * to end.
Row 2 K the knit sts and p the purl sts.
Rep row 2 for k1, p1 rib until piece measures approx 28"/71cm from beg. Do not bind off.
Counting from either side, place markers on the following sts: 16, 31, 46, and 61.

Gauge
28 sts and 27 rows to 4"/10cm over k1, p1 rib using size 6 (4mm) needles.
Take time to check gauge.

33

Ribbon Waves

Next row [Work in rib to marked st, remove marker and drop marked st to cast-on edge] 4 times, work to end in rib—72 sts. Leave last row on hold on needle. Cut ribbon into 4 equal lengths. Working along dropped-st columns, weave ribbon over 3 strands, then under 2 strands, along length of piece. Carefully remove provisional cast-on and place sts on needle. Join ends using 3-needle bind-off. With needle and thread, sew ribbon edges tog on WS and trim ends.■

94

34

Touch of Texture

A pattern using only knit and purl stitches is easy but looks stunning in a big cowl with bold color.

DESIGNED BY DEBBIE O'NEILL

Knitted Measurements
Circumference 26½"/67.5cm
Length 7½"/19cm

Materials
▨ 1 3½oz/100g hank (each approx 197yd/180m) of Cascade Yarns *Highland Duo* (baby alpaca/merino wool) in #2300 ruby ④
▨ Size 6 (4mm) circular needle, 24"/60cm long, *or size to obtain gauge*
▨ Stitch marker

Cowl
Cast on 132 sts. Join, taking care not to twist sts, and place marker for beg of rnd. Work in simple stitch pat until piece measures 7½"/19cm, end with a rnd 1. Bind off loosely knitwise.

Finishing
Block lightly. ■

Simple Stitch Pattern
(multiple of 4 sts)
Rnd 1 *P3, k1; rep from * around.
Rnds 2 and 4 Knit.
Rnd 3 *P1, k1, p2; rep from * around.
Rep rnds 1–4 for simple stitch pat.

Gauge
20 sts and 30 rnds to 4"/10cm over simple stitch pat using size 6 (4mm) needles.
Take time to check gauge.

35

Snug in Stripes

Fisherman's rib is worked in stripes on the diagonal in a reversible piece with a unique, modern shape.

DESIGNED BY ASHLEY RAO

Knitted Measurements
Circumference at lower edge
26"/66cm
Circumference at neck edge
18"/45.5cm
Length 7½"/19cm

Materials
▪ 1 3½oz/100g hank (each approx 197yd/180m) of Cascade Yarns *Highland Duo* (baby alpaca/merino wool) each in #2318 navy (MC) and #2303 grey (CC) (**4**)
▪ Size 3 (3.25mm) circular needle, 16"/40cm long, *or size to obtain gauge*
▪ Stitch markers

Note
A smaller needle is used to work the fisherman's rib for greater definition.

Stitch Glossary
K1-b Knit 1 in the row below the next st.
P1-b Purl 1 in the row below the next st.

Fisherman's Rib
(over an even number of sts)
Rnd 1 With CC, *k1-b, k1; rep from *

around.
Rnd 2 With MC, *p1, p1-b; rep from * around.
Rep rnds 1 and 2 for fisherman's rib.

Cowl
With MC, cast on 76 sts. Join, taking

care not to twist sts, and place marker (pm) for beg of rnd.
Set-up rnd With MC, p38, pm, p38. Beg with rnd 1, work in fisherman's rib for 24 rnds, end with a rnd 2.

BEGIN SHAPING
Rnd 1 With CC, *k1-b, k1; rep from * around.
Rnd 2 With MC, p1, *p1-b, p1; rep from * to 1 st before marker, (p1-b, yo, p1-b) in next st, sl marker, p1, (p1-b, yo, p1-b) in next st, **p1, p1-b; rep from ** to end of rnd—4 sts inc'd.
Rnd 3 With CC, k1-b, *k1, k1-b; rep from * to 3 sts before marker, k3, sl marker, k1-b, k3, **k1-b, k1; rep from ** to end of rnd.
Rnds 4–8 Work even in fisherman's rib. Rep rnds 1–8 seven times more—108 sts. Cut CC.

Bind-off rnd With MC, p1, k1-b, pass first st over and off RH needle, *p1, pass first st over and off RH needle, k1-b, pass first st over and off RH needle; rep from * around.

Finishing
Block lightly to measurements. ▪

Gauge
17 sts and 48 rnds to 4"/10cm over fisherman's rib using size 3 (3.25mm) needle.
Take time to check gauge.

36

Waves of Lace

An unusual lace pattern forms wavy bands of ribbing lightened by eyelets.

DESIGNED BY WEI WILKINS

Knitted Measurements
Circumference 48"/122cm
Length 6½"/6.5cm

Materials
■ 2 3½oz/100g hanks (each approx 197yd/180m) of Cascade Yarns *Highland Duo* (baby alpaca/merino wool) in #2303 grey (**4**)
■ One each sizes 6 and 8 (4 and 5mm) circular needles, 24"/60cm long, *or size to obtain gauge*
■ Stitch markers

Lace Pattern
(multiple of 12 sts)
Rnd 1 *[K1, p1] 3 times, k1, k2tog, p1, k1, p1, yo; rep from * around.
Rnd 2 *[K1, p1] 3 times, k2tog, p1, k1, p1, yo, p1; rep from * around.
Rnd 3 *[K1, p1] twice, k1, k2tog, p1, k1, p1, yo, k1, p1; rep from * around.
Rnd 4 *[K1, p1] twice, k2tog, p1, k1, p1, yo, p1, k1, p1; rep from * around.

Rnd 5 *K1, p1, k1, k2tog, p1, k1, p1, yo, [k1, p1] twice; rep from * around.
Rnd 6 *K1, p1, k2tog, p1, k1, p1, yo, [p1, k1] twice, p1; rep from * around.
Rnd 7 *K1, k2tog, p1, k1, p1, yo, [k1, p1] 3 times; rep from * around.
Rnd 8 *K2tog, p1, k1, p1, yo, [p1, k1] 3 times, p1; rep from * around.

Rnds 9 and 10 *K1, p1; rep from * around.
Rep rnds 1–10 for lace pattern.

Cowl
With smaller needle, cast on 300 sts. Join, taking care not to twist sts, and place marker for beg of rnd.
Rnd 1 *K1, p1; rep from * around.
Rep rnd 1 for k1, p1 rib once more.
Change to larger needle.
Work rnds 1–10 of lace pattern 4 times.
Change to smaller needle.
Work 1 rnd in k1, p1 rib. Bind off in rib. ■

Gauge
25 sts and 27 rnds to 4"/10cm over lace pattern using size 8 (5mm) needle.
Take time to check gauge.

Windswept Cables

A sandy neutral hue and wavy cable pattern evoke a windy day at the beach.

DESIGNED BY LARS RAINS

Knitted Measurements
Circumference 52"/132cm
Length 8"/20.5cm

Materials
- 2 3½oz/100g hanks (each approx 197yd/180m) of Cascade Yarns *Eco Duo* (baby alpaca/merino wool) in #1712 almond smoke (4)
- Size 8 (5mm) circular needle, 40"/100cm long, *or size to obtain gauge*
- Cable needle (cn)
- Stitch marker

Stitch Glossary
6-st RC Sl 3 sts to cn, hold to *back*, k3, k3 from cn.
6-st LC Sl 3 sts to cn, hold to *front*, k3, k3 from cn.

Sand Wind Pattern
(multiple of 12 sts)
Rnd 1 Knit.
Rnd 2 and all even-numbered rnds Knit.
Rnd 3 *6-st LC, k6; rep from * around.
Rnd 5 Knit.
Rnd 7 *K6, 6-st RC; rep from * around.
Rnd 8 Knit.
Rep rnds 1-8 for sand wind pat.

Cowl
Cast on 300 sts. Join, taking care not to twist sts, and place marker for beg of rnd.
Rnd 1 *K2, p2; rep from * around.
Rep rnd 1 for k2, p2 rib for 7 rnds more. Work rnds 1–8 of sand wind pat 5 times. Knit 1 rnd, then work in k2, p2 rib for 8 rnds. Bind off loosely in rib. ■

Gauge
23 sts and 32 rnds to 4"/10cm over sand wind pat using size 8 (5mm) needle.
Take time to check gauge.

Bands of Bold

Colorful zigzag bands separated by bright stripes make up
an eye-catching, shoulder-hugging design.

DESIGNED BY CHERYL MURRAY

Knitted Measurements
Circumference at neck edge 24"/61cm
Circumference at lower edge
44"/111.5cm
Length 12½"/31.5cm

Materials
1 3½oz/100g hank (each approx
164yd/150m) of Cascade Yarns *Cloud*
(merino wool/baby alpaca) each in
#2109 ruby (A) and #2135 turquoise
(B) (4)
1 3½oz/100g hank (each approx
164yd/150m) of Cascade Yarns *Eco
Cloud* (merino wool/baby alpaca) in
#1801 cream (C)
Size 10 (6mm) circular needle,
24"/60cm long, *or size to obtain gauge*
Stitch marker

Note
Cowl is worked from the neck edge
down.

Cowl
With A, cast on 120 sts. Join, taking care not
to twist sts, and place marker for beg of rnd.

BEGIN CHART
Rnd 1 Work 4-st rep 30 times around.
Cont to work chart in this manner
through rnd 5.
Rnd 6 With A, *k6, M1; rep from *
around—140 sts.
Work rnds 7–23, working 4-st rep 35

times around.
Rnd 24 With A, *k7, M1; rep from *
around—160 sts.
Work rnds 7–23, working 4-st rep 40
times around.
Rnd 24 With A, *k8, M1; rep from *
around—180 sts.
Work rnds 7–23, working 4-st rep 45
times around.
Rnd 24 With A, *k9, M1; rep from *
around—200 sts.
Work rnds 7–19, working 4-st rep 50
times around.
Rnd 20 With A, *k10, M1; rep from *
around—220 sts.
Work rnds 1–4, working 4-st rep 55
times around.
With A, bind off loosely. Block lightly to
measurements.■

Gauge
20 sts and 24 rnds to 4"/10cm over chart pat using size 10 (6mm) needle.
Take time to check gauge.

COLOR KEY
■ Ruby (A)
▨ Turquoise (B)
☐ Cream (C)

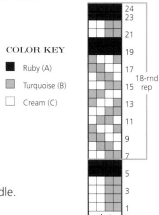

Frosted Flowers

An alternating pattern of eyelets and leaves evokes soft, snow-white blooms.

DESIGNED BY LARS RAINS

■■■▢

Knitted Measurements
Circumference at lower edge
43"/109cm
Length 6½"/16.5cm

Materials
■ 2 3½oz/100g hanks (each approx 197yd/180m) of Cascade Yarns *Eco Highland Duo* (baby alpaca/merino wool) in #2204 ecru (**4**)
■ One size 9 (5.5mm) circular needle, 24"/60cm long, *or size to obtain gauge*
■ Stitch marker

Frost Flowers Pattern
(multiple of 34 sts)
Rnd 1 *Yo, ssk, k2, yo, ssk, p2, yo, k4, ssk, k6, k2tog, k4, yo, p2, k2, yo, ssk, k2; rep from * around.
Rnd 2 *K2, k2tog, yo, k2, p2, k1, yo, k4, ssk, k4, k2tog, k4, yo, k1, p2, k2tog, yo, k2, k2tog, yo; rep from * around.
Rnd 3 *Yo, ssk, k2, yo, ssk, p2, k2, yo, k4, ssk, k2, k2tog, k4, yo, k2, p2, k2, yo, ssk, k2; rep from * around.
Rnd 4 *K2, k2tog, yo, k2, p2, k3, yo, k4, ssk, k2tog, k4, yo, k3, p2, k2tog, yo, k2, k2tog, yo; rep from * around.
Rnds 5–12 Rep rnds 1–4 twice more.

Rnd 13 *K3, k2tog, k4, yo, p2, [k2, yo, ssk] 3 times, p2, yo, k4, ssk, k3; rep from * around.
Rnd 14 *K2, k2tog, k4, yo, k1, p2, [k2tog, yo, k2] 3 times, p2, k1, yo, k4, ssk, k2; rep from * around.
Rnd 15 *K1, k2tog, k4, yo, k2, p2, [k2, yo, ssk] 3 times, p2, k2, yo, k4, ssk, k1; rep from * around.
Rnd 16 *K2tog, k4, yo, k3, p2, [k2tog, yo, k2] 3 times, p2, k3, yo, k4, ssk; rep from * around.

Rnds 17–24 Rep rnds 13–16 twice more.

Cowl
Using cable cast-on, cast on 170 sts. Join, taking care not to twist sts, and place marker for beg of rnd.

BEG FROST FLOWERS PATTERN
Note Pattern can be worked from text or chart.
Work rnds 1–24 of frost flowers pattern. Knit 12 rnds. Bind off loosely. ■

STITCH KEY
☐ k on RS, p on WS
⊟ p on RS, k on WS
☒ k2tog
☒ ssk
◎ yo

34-st rep

Gauge
16 sts and 24 rnds to 4"/10cm over St st using size 9 (5.5mm) needles.
Take time to check gauge.

Buttoned Up

Have fun choosing snazzy statement buttons to personalize a chunky cabled cowl.

DESIGNED BY LINDA MEDINA

Knitted Measurements
Circumference (buttoned) 30"/76cm
Width 9"/23cm

Materials
- 2 3½oz/100g hanks (each approx 164yd/150m) of Cascade Yarns *Cloud* (merino wool/baby alpaca) in #2132 peacock green (4)
- One pair size 10 (6mm) needles *or size to obtain gauge*
- One each sizes 7 and 8 (4.5 and 5mm) circular needles, 24"/60cm long
- Stitch markers
- Cable needle (cn)
- Four 1"/25mm buttons

One-Row Buttonhole
Note: This buttonhole technique uses 5 sts to make a 4-st buttonhole.
Bring yarn to front of work and sl next st purlwise. Move yarn to back of work and leave it there. *Sl next st from LH needle purlwise, pass the first slipped st over; rep from * 3 times more. Sl the last st

back to the LH needle and turn work. Using the cable cast-on, cast on 5 sts, turn. Sl the first st wyib, pass the extra cast-on st over it to close the buttonhole.

Stitch Glossary
Drop st and yo Drop st from LH needle and let it unravel to yo below, yo to make a new st.
11-st RC Sl 6 sts to cn, hold to *back*, k2, p1, k2, then work sts from cn as foll: [p1, k2] twice.

Cowl
With size 10 (6mm) needles, cast on 45 sts.
Row 1 (RS) P1, *k1, p1; rep from * to end.
Row 2 K the knit sts and p the purl sts.
Rep rows 1 and 2 once for k1, p1 rib, then rep row 1 once more.
Set-up row (WS) K4, [p2, k1] 3 times, p2, k2, [p1, p2tog, yo] 3 times, p2, k2, [p2, k1] 3 times, p2, k4.

BEG CHART
Work rows 1–24 of chart 7 times.
Next row (RS) P1, *k1, p1; rep from * to end.
Next row (WS) K the knit sts and p the purl sts.
Next (buttonhole) row (RS) P1, k1, [work 1-row buttonhole, work 7 sts in rib] 3 times, work 1-row buttonhole, work to end in rib.
Work 2 rows more in rib. Bind off in rib. Block lightly.

Gauge
26 sts and 23 rows to 4"/10cm over chart pat using size 10 (6mm) needles.
Take time to check gauge.

Buttoned Up

EDGING

With RS facing and larger circular needle, pick up and k 168 sts evenly along one side edge.

Row 1 (WS) *K1, p1; rep from * to end.
Row 2 K the knit sts and p the purl sts.
Rep row 2 for k1, p1 rib for 3 rows more. With smaller circular needle, bind off in rib.
Repeat for opposite side edge.
Sew buttons approx 3 rows from cast-on edge to correspond to buttonholes.■

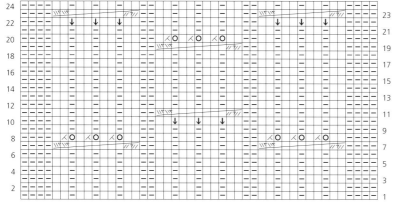

45 sts

STITCH KEY

☐ k on RS, p on WS

— p on RS, k on WS

O yo

⤫ p2tog

↓ drop st and yo

⟋⟋⟍⟋⟍ 11-st RC

41

Curled Up in Cables

Cables alternate with dropped stitches in a piece
that's oversized enough to wear as a snuggly snood.

DESIGNED BY ASHLEY RAO

■■■□

Knitted Measurements
Circumference 33"/83.5cm
Length (after assembly) Approx
27"/68.5cm

Materials
■ 4 3½oz/100g hanks (each approx
164yd/150m) of Cascade Yarns *Cloud*
(merino wool/baby alpaca) in #2105
pumpkin (**4**)
■ One pair size 10½ (6.5mm) needles *or
size to obtain gauge*
■ Cable needle (cn)
■ Stitch marker

Stitch Glossary
2-st RC Sl 1 st to cn and hold to *back*,
k1, k1 from cn.
2-st RC-inc Sl 1 st to cn and hold to
back, kfb, M1, k1 from cn—2 sts inc'd.
4-st RC Sl 2 sts to cn and hold to *back*,
k2, k2 from cn.
4-st RC-inc Sl 2 sts to cn and hold to
back, k1, kfb, M1, k2 from cn—2 sts
inc'd.
4-st RC-dec Sl 2 sts to cn and hold to
back, ssk; k2tog from cn—2 sts dec'd.
6-st RC Sl 3 sts to cn and hold to *back*,
k3, k3 from cn.

6-st RC-inc Sl 3 sts to cn and hold to
back, k2, kfb, M1, k3 from cn—2 sts
inc'd.
6-st RC-dec Sl 3 sts to cn and hold to
back, k1, ssk; k2tog, k1 from cn—2 sts
dec'd.
8-st RC Sl 4 sts to cn and hold to *back*,
k4, k4 from cn.

8-st RC-dec Sl 4 sts to cn and hold to
back, k2, ssk; k2tog, k2 from cn—2 sts
dec'd.
10-st RC Sl 5 sts to cn and hold to *back*,
k5, k5 from cn.
10-st RC-dec Sl 5 sts to cn and hold to back,
k3, ssk; k2tog, k3 from cn—2 sts dec'd.

Slipped Stockinette Stitch
Row 1 (RS) Knit.
Row 2 Sl 1, p to end.
Rep rows 1 and 2 for slipped St st.

Notes
1) Cowl is made up of 2 drop st cable
panels. Each is worked flat and grafted
to form a tube; they are sewn together
to form the cowl.
2) Stitches in each drop st cable panel
are dropped when the panel is complete.

Cowl
DROP STITCH CABLE PANEL (MAKE 2)
Cast on 24 sts. Purl 1 row.
Row 1 (RS) Knit.
**Row 2 and all even-numbered rows
(WS)** Sl 1, p to end.
Row 3 [2-st RC, k1] 8 times.
Row 4 Rep row 2.

Gauge
16 sts and 24 rows to 4"/10cm over St st using size 10½ (6.5mm) needles.
Take time to check gauge.

Curled Up in Cables

Rep last 2 rows twice more.
Next row (RS) [2-st RC-inc, k1] 8 times—40 sts.
Work 3 rows in slipped St st.
Next row [4-st RC, k1] 8 times.
Work 3 rows in slipped St st.
Rep last 4 rows once more.
Next row (RS) [4-st RC-inc, k1] 8 times—56 sts.
Work 5 rows in slipped St st.
Next row (RS) [6-st RC, k1] 8 times.
Work 5 rows in slipped St st.

Rep last 6 rows once more.
Next row (RS) [6-st RC-inc, k1] 8 times—72 sts.
Work 7 rows in slipped St st.
Next row (RS) [8-st RC, k1] 8 times.
Work 7 rows in slipped St st.
Rep last 8 rows once more.
Next row (RS) [8-st RC-inc, k1] 8 times across—88 sts.
Work 9 rows in slipped St st.
Next row (RS) [10-st RC, k1] 8 times across.

Work 9 rows in slipped St st.
Rep last 10 rows once more.
Next row (RS) [10-st RC-dec, k1] 8 times across—72 sts.
Work 7 rows in slipped St st.
Next row (RS) [8-st RC, k1] 8 times across.
Work 7 rows in slipped St st.
Rep last 8 rows once more.
Next row (RS) [8-st RC-dec, k1] 8 times across—56 sts.
Work 5 rows in slipped St st.
Next row (RS) [6-st RC, k1] 8 times across.
Work 5 rows in slipped St st.
Rep last 6 rows once more.
Next row (RS) [6-st RC-dec, k1] 8 times across—40 sts.
Work 3 rows in slipped St st.
Next row (RS) [4-st RC, k1] 8 times across.
Rep last 4 rows once more.
Next row (RS) [4-st RC-dec] 8 times across—24 sts.
Next row Sl 1, p to end.
Next row (RS) [2-st RC, k1] 8 times across.
Rep last 2 rows once more.
Next row (WS) *Sl 2, drop next st; rep from * to last 3 sts, sl 3. Be sure that all sts drop to cast-on edge. Sew open sts of cables to corresponding sts in cast-on edge to form tube. Place a marker in seam edge.

Finishing
Place markers in edge of each tube opposite the seam markers to mark the center of the group of 10-st cables. With the seam marker of first tube matching the center marker of the 2nd tube, and vice versa, sew the tubes together. ∎

Zigzag Ridges

A chevron motif that extends to the zigzag edges lends a modern, geometric look to a soft autumnal hue.

DESIGNED BY DEBBIE O'NEILL

Knitted Measurements
Circumference 23"/58.5cm
Length 8½"/21.5cm

Materials
▨ 1 3½oz/100g hank (each approx 197yd/180m) of Cascade Yarns *Eco Duo* (baby alpaca/merino wool) in #1704 chicory (4)
▨ Size 6 (4mm) circular needle, 20"/50cm long, *or size to obtain gauge*
▨ Stitch marker

Rep rnds 1–12 for zigzag ridges pat.

Cowl
Cast on 126 sts. Join, taking care not to twist sts, and place marker for beg of rnd. Work rnds 1–12 of zigzag ridges pattern 4 times, then work rnds 1–10 once more.
Bind off loosely.

Finishing
Block lightly.■

Zigzag Ridges Pattern
(multiple of 14 sts)
Rnds 1, 3, 5, 7, and 9 Knit.
Rnds 2, 4, 6, 8, and 10 *Yo, k3, ssk, yo, SK2P, yo, k2tog, k3, yo, k1; rep from * around.
Rnds 11 and 12 Purl.

Gauge
22 sts and 28 rnds to 4"/10cm over zigzag ridges pat using size 6 (4mm) needle.
Take time to check gauge.

43

Gather 'Round

Bands of seed stitch alternate with ruching for a beautiful balance of structure and shape.

DESIGNED BY KATHERINE MEHLS

Knitted Measurements
Circumference 48"/122cm
Length 10"/25.5cm

Materials
■ 4 3½oz/100g hanks (each approx 164yd/150m) of Cascade Yarns *Cloud* (merino wool/baby alpaca) in #2123 dark periwinkle (④)
■ One pair size 10½ (6.5mm) needles *or size to obtain gauge*
■ Stitch markers

Cowl
Cast on 40 sts.
**Row 1 (RS) *K1, p1; rep from * to end.
Row 2 K the purl sts and p the knit sts.

Rep row 2 for seed stitch for 10 rows more, end with a WS row.
Increase row (RS) *Kfb; rep from * to end—80 sts.
Next row (WS) Purl.
Cont in St st (k on RS, p on WS) for 2"/5cm, end with a WS row.
Decrease row (RS) *K2tog; rep from * to end—40 sts.
Next row Purl.**

Rep between **'s 11 times more.
Next row (RS) Knit.
Bind off on WS. Sew ends together to form cowl.■

Gauge
16 sts and 24 rows to 4"/10cm over St st using size 10½ (6.5mm) needles.
Take time to check gauge.

Cozy Quilted

An easy-to-make diamond knit and purl pattern
subtly evokes the charm of quilted fabric.

DESIGNED BY COURTNEY CEDARHOLM

■■□□

Knitted Measurements
Circumference 64"/162.5cm
Length 9"/23cm

Materials
■ 3 3½oz/100g hanks (each approx
164yd/150m) of Cascade Yarns *Eco
Cloud* (merino wool/baby alpaca) in
#1801 cream (**4**)
■ Size 9 (5.5mm) circular needle,
40"/100cm long, *or size to obtain gauge*
■ Stitch markers

Note
Pattern may be worked from text or
chart.

Stitch Pattern
(over a multiple of 18 sts)
Rnds 1 and 2 *K5, p8, k5; rep from *
around.
Rnds 3 and 4 *K4, p4, k2, p4, k4; rep
from * around.
Rnds 5 and 6 *K3, p4, k4, p4, k3; rep
from * around.
Rnds 7 and 8 *K2, p4, k6, p4, k2; rep
from * around.

Rnds 9 and 10 *K1, p4, k8, p4, k1; rep
from * around.
Rnds 11 and 12 *P4, k10, p4; rep from
* around.
Rnds 13 and 14 Rep rnds 9 and 10.
Rnds 15 and 16 Rep rnds 7 and 8.
Rnds 17 and 18 Rep rnds 5 and 6.

Rnds 19 and 20 Rep rnds 3 and 4.
Rep rnds 1–20 for stitch pattern.

Cowl
Cast on 270 sts. Join, taking care not to
twist sts, and place marker for beg of
rnd.
Rnd 1 *K2, p2; rep from * around, end K2.
Rep rnd 1 for k2, p2 rib for 6 rnds more.
Work rnds 1–20 of pattern stitch twice.
Work in k2, p2 rib for 7 rnds.
Bind off in pat.■

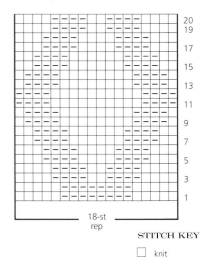

18-st
rep

STITCH KEY

□ knit
⊟ purl

Gauge
18 sts and 24 rnds to 4"/10cm over St st using size 9 (5.5mm) needle.
Take time to check gauge.

45

It's a Draw

Two crochet-chain drawstrings in a sweet eyelet-patterned cowl allow for a multitude of styling possibilities.

DESIGNED BY KIM HAESEMEYER

Knitted Measurements
Circumference 58"/147cm
Length 11½"/29cm

Materials
▧ 3 3½oz/100g hanks (each approx 197yd/180m) of Cascade Yarns *Highland Duo* (baby alpaca/merino wool) in #2301 burgundy (4)
▧ One pair size 9 (5.5mm) needles *or size to obtain gauge*
▧ One extra size 9 (5.5mm) needle for 3-needle bind-off
▧ Size I/9 (5.5mm) crochet hook
▧ Scrap yarn of similar weight to working yarn for provisional cast-on

Pattern Stitch
(multiple of 12 sts plus 2)
Row 1 (RS) Knit.
Row 2 Purl.
Row 3 K4, k2tog, k1, yo, *k9, k2tog, k1, yo; rep from * to last 7 sts, k7.
Row 4 P8, yo, p1, p2tog, *p9, yo, p1, p2tog; rep from * to last 3 sts, p3.
Row 5 K2, *k2tog, k1, yo, k9; rep from * to end.
Row 6 P10, yo, p1, p2tog, *p9, yo, p1, p2tog; rep from * to last st, p1.
Row 7 Knit.
Row 8 Purl.
Row 9 K7, yo, k1, SKP, *k9, yo, k1, SKP; rep from * to last 4 sts, k4.
Row 10 P3, p2tog tbl, p1, yo, *p9, p2tog tbl, p1, yo; rep from * to last 8 sts, p8.
Row 11 *K9, yo, k1, SKP; rep from * to last 2 sts, k2.
Row 12 P1, p2tog tbl, p1, yo, *p9, p2tog tbl, p1, yo; rep from * to last 10 sts, p10.
Rep rows 1–12 for pattern stitch.

Provisional Cast-On
Using scrap yarn and crochet hook, chain the number of sts to cast on, plus a few extra. Cut a tail and pull the tail through the last chain. With knitting needle and yarn, pick up and knit the stated number of sts through the "purl bumps" on the back of the chain. To remove scrap chain, when instructed, pull out the tail from the last crochet st. Gently and slowly pull on the tail to unravel the crochet sts, carefully placing each released knit st on a needle.

3-Needle Bind-Off
1) Hold right sides of pieces together on 2 needles. Insert 3rd needle knitwise into

Gauge
19 sts and 25 rows to 4"/10cm over pat st using size 9 (5.5mm) needles.
Take time to check gauge.

It's a Draw

first st of each needle and wrap yarn knitwise.

2) Knit these 2 sts together and slip them off the needles. *Knit the next 2 sts together in the same manner.

3) Slip first st on 3rd needle over 2nd st and off needle. Rep from * in step 2 across row until all sts are bound off.

Cowl
Cast on 56 sts using provisional cast-on.
Set up row (WS) K3, p to last 3 sts, k3.

BEG PATTERN STITCH
Row 1 (RS) K3 (garter st selvage sts), work row 1 of pattern stitch to last 3 sts, k3 (garter st selvage sts).
Row 2 (WS) K3, work row 2 of pattern stitch to last 3 sts, k3.
Cont to work pattern stitch in this way, keeping 3 sts at each edge in garter stitch, until rows 1–12 of pattern stitch have been worked 30 times.
Carefully remove provisional cast-on and join cast-on edge to last row using 3-needle bind-off. Block gently to measurements.
With hook, make two 65"/165cm chains. Working into center 2 reps of pattern stitch, weave chains in and out of eyelets in rows 3 and 9. Gather strands and tie, using photo as guide.■

Cables on the Edge

Traditional design elements get a fresh twist: ribs in the middle are flanked by cables at the edges.

DESIGNED BY CHERYL MURRAY

Knitted Measurements
Circumference 60"/152.5cm
Length 8½"/21.5cm

Materials
■ 3 3½oz/100g hanks (each approx 197yd/180m) of Cascade Yarns *Eco Duo* (baby alpaca/merino wool) in #1711 caramel cream (■4■)
■ One pair size 8 (5mm) needles *or size to obtain gauge*
■ Additional size 8 (5mm) needle for 3-needle bind-off
■ Size H/8 (5mm) crochet hook and scrap yarn for provisional cast-on
■ Cable needle (cn)

Provisional Cast-On
Using scrap yarn and crochet hook, chain the number of sts to cast on, plus a few extra. Cut a tail and pull the tail through the last chain. With knitting needle and yarn, pick up and knit the stated number of sts through the "purl bumps" on the back of the chain. To remove scrap chain, when instructed, pull out the tail from the last crochet st. Gen-

tly and slowly pull on the tail to unravel the crochet sts, carefully placing each released knit st on a needle.

3-Needle Bind-Off
1) Hold right sides of pieces together on 2 needles. Insert 3rd needle knitwise into first st of each needle and wrap yarn

knitwise.
2) Knit these 2 sts together and slip them off the needles. *Knit the next 2 sts together in the same manner.
3) Slip first st on 3rd needle over 2nd st and off needle. Rep from * in step 2 across row until all sts are bound off.

Stitch Glossary
4-st RC Sl 2 sts to cn, hold to *back*, k2, k2 from cn.
4-st LC Sl 2 sts to cn, hold to *front*, k2, k2 from cn.
4-st RPC Sl 2 sts to cn, hold to *back*, k2, p2 from cn.
4-st LPC Sl 2 sts to cn, hold to *front*, p2, k2 from cn.

Cowl
Cast on 51 sts using provisional cast-on method.
Beg with a WS row, rep rows 1–8 of chart until piece measures 60"/152.5cm from beg, end with a row 1 of chart.

Finishing
Carefully remove sts from provisional cast-on and join first row to last row with 3-needle bind-off. Block lightly.■

Gauge
18 sts and 26 rows to 4"/10cm over St st using size 8 (5mm) needles.
Take time to check gauge.

Cables on the Edge

46

STITCH KEY

☐ k on RS, p on

⊟ p on RS, k on

▨ 4-st R(

▨ 4-st L(

▨ 4-st RF

▨ 4-st LF

51 sts

8 6 4 2

7 5 3 1 (WS)

Horseshoe Cables

A bold band of cables at one edge is enough to make a seed stitch cowl into a show-stopper.

DESIGNED BY DEBORAH HELMKE

Knitted Measurements
Circumference at cabled edge
32"/81cm
Length 14"/35.5cm

Materials
- 2 3½oz/100g hanks (each approx 197yd/180m) of Cascade Yarns *Eco Duo* (baby alpaca/merino wool) in #1710 pecan whip (4)
- One pair size 8 (5mm) needles *or size to obtain gauge*
- Size 8 (5mm) circular needle, 24"/60cm long
- Cable needle (cn)
- Stitch marker

Stitch Glossary
10-st RC Sl 5 sts to cn, hold to *back,* k5, k5 from cn.
10-st LC Sl 5 sts to cn, hold to *front,* k5, k5 from cn.

Cable Pattern
(over 31 sts)
Rows 1, 5, 7, and 11 (RS) Knit.
Row 2 and all WS rows Purl.
Row 3 K10, 10-st RC, 10-st LC, k1.
Row 9 10-st LC, k20, k1.
Row 12 Purl.
Rep rows 1–12 for cable pat.

Note
Cable band is worked first, then body of cowl is picked up along edge of cable band.

Cowl
With straight needles, cast on 31 sts. Work rows 1–12 of cable pat until piece measures 32"/81cm from beg, end with a row 12. Bind off.
With RS facing and circular needle, pick up and k 130 sts along left side edge of cable panel. Do not join, work back and forth in rows as foll:
Row 1 (RS) *K1, p1; rep from * to end.
Row 2 K the purl sts and p the knit sts.
Rep row 2 for seed stitch for 2 rows more.
Next (dec) row K2tog, work in seed stitch to last 2 sts, k2tog—2 sts dec'd.
Rep dec row every 5th row 13 times more—102 sts.
Bind off in pat.
Sew back seam.■

Gauge
16 sts and 28 rows to 4"/10cm over seed st using size 9 (5.5mm) needles.
Take time to check gauge.

Budding Out

A chunky cable on one side and picot edge on the other
creatively frame a pattern of pretty buds.

DESIGNED BY STEVEN HICKS

Knitted Measurements
Circumference 48"/122cm
Length 8"/20.5cm

Materials
■ 2 3½oz/100g hanks (each approx
197yd/180m) of Cascade Yarns *Highland
Duo* (alpaca/merino wool) in #2307
beet
■ Size 9 (5.5mm) circular needle,
24"/60cm long, *or size to obtain gauge*
■ Cable needle (cn)
■ Size I/9 (5.5mm) crochet hook for
provisional cast-on
■ Scrap yarn
■ Stitch marker

Stitch Glossary
8-st RC Sl 4 sts to cn and hold to *back*,
k4, k4 from cn.
8-st LC Sl 4 sts to cn and hold to *front*,
k4, k4 from cn.

Provisional Cast-On
Using scrap yarn and crochet hook,
chain the number of sts to cast on, plus
a few extra. Cut a tail and pull the tail
through the last chain. With knitting needle

and yarn, pick up and knit the stated number of sts through the "purl bumps" on the
back of the chain. To remove scrap chain,
when instructed, pull out the tail from the
last crochet st. Gently and slowly pull on the
tail to unravel the crochet sts, carefully placing each released knit st on a needle.

Note
Cable edge is worked in rows first and
grafted tog to form a tube. Sts are
picked up along the cable edge to work
the main cowl.

Cable Strip
Cast on 18 sts using provisional cast-on.
Rows 1, 3, and 5 (RS) Knit.
Rows 2, 4, and 6 Purl.
Row 7 (RS) K2, 8-st RC, 8-st LC.
Row 8 Purl.
Rep rows 1–8 for 28 times more, then
rep rows 1–7 once. Cut yarn.
Carefully remove scrap yarn from provi-
sional cast-on and place open sts on a
needle. Graft ends tog.

Main Cowl
With RS facing, pick up and k 160 sts
along edge of cable strip (approx 2 sts

for every 3 rows). Join and place marker
for beg of rnd.
Next (dec) rnd [P38, p2tog] 4 times
around—156 sts.

BEG PATTERN STITCH
Note Stitch count changes when work-
ing pat st.
Rnds 1–3 Purl.
Rnd 4 *P1, k into st 3 rnds below next
st, yo, k same st 3 rows below, then drop
st from LH needle, p4; rep from *
around.
Rnd 5 *P1, k3, p4; rep from * around.
Rnd 6 *P1, S2KP, p4; rep from * around.
Rnds 7–9 Purl.
Rnd 10 *P4, k into st 3 rnds below next
st, yo, k same st 3 rows below, then drop
st from LH needle, p1; rep from *
around.
Rnd 11 *P4, k3, p1; rep from * around.
Rnd 12 *P4, S2KP, p1; rep from * around.
Rep rnds 1–12 once more, then rnds 1–8
once.
Knit 4 rnds.
Picot bind-off rnd Bind off 2 sts, *sl st
from RH needle back to LH needle, cast
on 2 sts, bind off 4 sts; rep from * until
all sts are bound off.■

Gauge
13 sts and 24 rounds to 4"/10cm over pat st using size 9 (5.5mm) needles.
Take time to check gauge.

49

Pixelation

Wide pixelated stripes on a tubular cowl are on trend,
especially in modern black and white.

DESIGNED BY MATTHEW SCHRANK

Knitted Measurements
Circumference 38"/96.5cm
Length 8½"/21.5cm

Materials
■ 2 3½oz/100g hanks (each approx
220yd/201m) of Cascade Yarns *Highland
Duo* (baby alpaca/merino wool) in #2302
black (A) (**4**)
■ 2 3½oz/100g hanks (each approx
220yd/201m) of Cascade Yarns *Eco
Highland Duo* (baby alpaca/merino wool)
in #2204 ecru (B) (**4**)
■ Size 8 (5mm) circular needle,
16"/40cm long, *or size to obtain gauge*
■ Size H/8 (5mm) crochet hook and
scrap yarn for provisional cast-on
■ Stitch marker

Provisional Cast-On
Using scrap yarn and crochet hook,
chain the number of sts to cast on, plus
a few extra. Cut a tail and pull the tail
through the last chain. With knitting
needle and yarn, pick up and knit the
stated number of sts through the "purl

bumps" on the back of the chain. To remove scrap chain, when instructed, pull
out the tail from the last crochet st. Gently and slowly pull on the tail to unravel
the crochet sts, carefully placing each
released knit st on a needle.

Cowl
With A, cast on 92 sts using provisional
cast-on method. Join, taking care not to
twist sts, and place marker
for beg of rnd.

BEG CHART
Rnd 1 Work 4-st chart 23
times around.
Cont to work chart in this
manner until rows 1–53 of
have been worked 4 times.
Carefully remove sts from
provisional cast-on and
graft last row to first row.■

COLOR KEY
▨ A
□ B

Gauge
22 sts and 22 rnds to 4"/10cm over chart pat using size 8 (5mm) needles.
Take time to check gauge.

4-st
rep

Woven with Care

A delicate woven stitch creates a basketweave look that perfectly shows off tonal variegation.

DESIGNED BY VANESSA PUTT

Knitted Measurements
Circumference 28"/71cm
Length 10"/25.5cm

Materials
▨ 1 3½oz/100g hanks (each approx 164yd/150m) of Cascade Yarns *Cloud* (merino wool/baby alpaca) in #2125 blue Hawaii and #2135 real teal 【4】
▨ Size 8 (5mm) circular needle, 24"/60cm long, *or size to obtain gauge*
▨ Cable needle (cn)
▨ Stitch marker

Cowl
With A, cast on 120 sts. Join, taking care not to twist sts, and place marker for beg of rnd. [Purl 1 rnd, knit 1 rnd] twice, purl 1 rnd.
Next rnd *K2, M1; rep from * around—180 sts.
Work in woven pat for 40 rnds. Change to A and cut B.
Next rnd *K1, k2tog; rep from * around—120 sts.
[Knit 1 rnd, purl 1 rnd] twice, knit 1 rnd. Bind off.

Finishing
Block to measurements. If desired, sew up the slight gaps at the round joinings.■

Woven Pattern
(multiple of 6 sts)
Rnd 1 With B, *k1 wrapping yarn twice around needle; rep from * around.
Rnd 2 With A, and letting extra yo drop when working each st, *sl 3 sts to cn and hold to *back*, k3, then k3 from cn; rep from * around.
Rnd 3 With A, *k1 wrapping yarn twice around needle; rep from * around.
Rnd 4 With B, and letting extra yo drop when working each st, k3, *sl 3 sts to cn and hold to *front*, k3, then k3 from cn; rep from * around, ending with k3.
Rep rnds 1–4 for woven pat.

Gauge
26 sts and 18 rnds to 4"/10cm over woven pat using size 8 (5mm) needle.
Take time to check gauge.

51

Stepped-Up Stripes

Have fun with color or go softly tonal with a cowl
that's tall and tubular for maximum warmth.

DESIGNED BY LISA SILVERMAN

Knitted Measurements
Circumference 24"/61cm
Length 8½"/21cm

Materials
■ 1 3½oz/100g hank (each approx
164yd/150m) of Cascade Yarns *Cloud*
(merino wool/baby alpaca) each in #2119
navy (A), #2135 turquoise (B), #2115
raspberry (C), and #2123 dark periwinkle
(D) (4)
■ Size 10 (6mm) circular needle,
24"/60cm long, *or size to obtain gauge*
■ Stitch marker
■ Size J/10 (6mm) crochet hook and
scrap yarn for provisional cast-on

Provisional Cast-On
Using scrap yarn and crochet hook,
chain the number of sts to cast on, plus
a few extra. Cut a tail and pull the tail
through the last chain. With knitting
needle and yarn, pick up and knit the
stated number of sts through the "purl
bumps" on the back of the chain. To remove scrap chain, when instructed, pull
out the tail from the last crochet st. Gently and slowly pull on the tail to unravel
the crochet sts, carefully placing each
released knit st on a needle.

Broken Stripe Pattern
(multiple of 6 sts)
Rnds 1 and 2 With A, knit.
Rnds 3 and 4 *With A, k3, with B, k3;
rep from * around.
Rnds 5 and 6 With B, knit.
Rnds 7 and 8 With C, knit.
Rnds 9 and 10 *With C, k3, with D, k3;
rep from * around.
Rnds 11 and 12 With D, knit.
Rep rnds 1–12 for broken stripe pat.

Cowl
Cast on 78 sts using provisional cast-on
method. Join, taking care not to twist
sts, and place marker for beg of rnd.
Work rnds 2–12 of broken stripe pat,
then work rnds 1–12 ten times, then
work rnds 1–11 once more.
Carefully remove provisional cast-on and
place sts on needle. With D, graft ends
together.■

Gauge
18 sts and 24 rows to 4"/10cm over St st using size 10 (6mm) needles.
Take time to check gauge.

52

Fishtail Cables

Small allover cables framed by ribbed edges create a textured fabric without too much bulk.

DESIGNED BY DORCAS SOKOLOW

Knitted Measurements
Circumference 25"/63cm
Length 11"/28cm

Materials
■ 2 3½oz/100g hanks (each approx 197yd/180m) of Cascade Yarns *Highland Duo* (baby alpaca/merino wool) in #2320 sparkling grape (**4**)
■ One each sizes 6 and 8 (4 and 5mm) circular needles, each 24"/60cm long, *or size to obtain gauge*
■ Cable needle (cn)
■ Stitch marker

Stitch Glossary
4-st RC Sl 2 sts to cn, hold to *back*, k2, k2 from cn.
4-st LC Sl 2 sts to cn, hold to *front*, k2, k2 from cn.

Fishtail Pattern
(over a multiple of 8 sts)
Rnds 1 and 3 Knit.
Rnd 2 *4-st RC, k4; rep from * around.
Rnd 4 *K4, 4-st LC; rep from * around.
Rep rnds 1–4 for fishtail pat.

Cowl
With smaller needle, cast on 160 sts. Join, taking care not to twist sts, and place marker for beg of rnd.
Rnd 1 *K1, p1; rep from * around.
Rep rnd 1 for k1, p1 rib for 1"/2.5cm. Change to larger needle.
Work in fishtail pattern until piece measures 10"/25.5cm from beg. Change to smaller needle. Work in k1, p1 rib for 1"/2.5cm. Bind off in rib.■

Gauge
26 sts and 28 rnds to 4"/10cm over fishtail pat using larger needles.
Take time to check gauge.

53

Zip It Up

The addition of two decorative zippers adds a sleek, modern edge to a soft, warm piece.

DESIGNED BY LORNA MISER

Knitted Measurements
Circumference (untwisted) approx 34"/86.5cm
Length 6½"/16.5cm

Materials
- 2 3½oz/100g hanks (each approx 197yd/180m) of Cascade Yarns *Eco Duo* (baby alpaca/merino wool) in #1713 moccasin (4)
- One set (5) size 8 (5mm) double-pointed needles *or size to obtain gauge*
- Size H/8 (5mm) crochet hook and scrap yarn in similar weight to working yarn for provisional cast-on
- Stitch marker
- Two 14"/35.5cm separating zippers
- Needle and matching thread

Provisional Cast-On
Using scrap yarn and crochet hook, ch the number of sts to cast on plus a few extra. Cut a tail and pull the tail through the last chain. With knitting needle and yarn, pick up and knit the stated number of sts through the "purl bumps" on the back of the chain. To remove scrap yarn chain, when instructed, pull out the tail

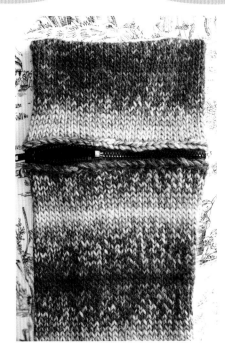

from the last crochet stitch. Gently and slowly pull on the tail to unravel the crochet stitches, carefully placing each released knit stitch on a needle.

Note
Cowl is constructed from two pieces, worked in the round and joined with

zippers. A provisional cast-on is used to create identical bound-off edges. Pieces may be zipped into a Mobius shape, if desired.

Cowl
LONG PIECE
Cast on 60 sts using provisional cast-on. Join, taking care not to twist sts, and place marker for beg of rnd. Work in St st (k every rnd) until piece measures 24"/61cm from beg. Bind off. Carefully remove cast-on and place sts on needles, bind off.

SHORT PIECE
Work as for long piece until piece measures 10"/25.5cm. Bind off. Carefully remove cast-on and place sts on needles, bind off.

Finishing
Block pieces to measurements. Overlap ends of zipper tape so pull fits against stopper, forming a ring, and sew overlapped tape. Pin zipper tape along edge of long piece, easing edge to fit along zipper tape and allowing teeth of zipper to show. Pin edge of smaller piece along opposite side of tape. Sew zipper in place. Repeat for second zipper and opposite ends of pieces. ■

Gauge
18 sts and 22 rnds to 4"/10cm over St st using size 8 (5mm) needle.
Take time to check gauge.

Faux Cables

Ribbed edges flow into cables created not by crossing,
but by wrapping ribbed sections together.

DESIGNED BY KIM HAESEMEYER

■■□▷

Knitted Measurements
Circumference, after wrapping
approx 54"/137cm
Length 7"/18cm

Materials
▪ 3 3½oz/100g hanks (each approx
197yd/180m) of Cascade Yarns *Highland
Duo* (baby alpaca/merino wool) in #2323
green spruce (**4**)
▪ Size 9 (5.5mm) circular needle,
40"/100cm long, *or size to obtain gauge*
▪ Stitch marker
▪ Tapestry needle

Note
Ribbed sections are wrapped together in
finishing to create gathered cables.

Cowl
Cast on 384 sts. Join, taking care not to
twist sts, and place marker for beg of rnd.
Rnd 1 *[K1 tbl] twice, p2; rep from *
around.
Rep rnd 1 for k2 tbl, p2 rib for 2"/5cm.

BEG BODY RIB
Next rnd *[K1 tbl] twice, p6; rep from *
around.
Rep last rnd for body rib for 20 rnds
more.
Work in k2 tbl, p2 rib for 2"/5cm. Bind
off in rib.

Finishing
Block and allow to dry.
Cut a strand of yarn long enough to
wrap sts along one entire round. Thread
strand through tapestry needle and
"wrap" sections of sts tog, wrapping
yarn around each section twice, pulling
sts tog to gather and carrying strand
across WS, as foll:
Rnd 1 of body rib Beg with the first st
of rnd 1, *wrap 10 sts, skip 2 purl sts;
rep from * around.
Rnd 11 of body rib (center rnd) Beg
with the 9th st from beg of rnd 11,
*wrap 10 sts, skip 6 purl sts; rep from *
around. (Note that these wraps will pull
knit ribs into X shapes.)
Rnd 21 of body rib Beg with the first st
of rnd 21, *wrap 10 sts, skip 6 purl sts;
rep from * around. (Note that these
wraps will gather the opposite rib
pairings of previous wrap round.)■

Gauge
18 sts and 24 rnds to 4"/10cm over St st using size 9 (5.5mm) needle.
Take time to check gauge.

55

Braided Beauty

Make a few of these easy braids of three stockinette strips
and stack them for extra substance and style.

DESIGNED BY CAROL J. SULCOSKI

■■□□

Knitted Measurements
Circumference 24"/61cm
Width (braided) approx 2"/5cm

Materials
■ 1 3½oz/100g hank (each approx
197yd/180m) of Cascade Yarns
Eco Duo (baby alpaca/merino wool) in
#1702 pecan (4)

■ One pair size 8 (5mm) needles *or size
to obtain gauge*

■ Spare size 8 (5mm) needle for 3-needle
bind-off

■ Size H/8 (5mm) crochet hook and scrap
yarn for provisional cast-on

■ Stitch markers

■ Stitch holders

Provisional Cast-On
Using scrap yarn and crochet hook,
chain the number of sts to cast on, plus
a few extra. Cut a tail and pull the tail
through the last chain. With knitting
needle and yarn, pick up and knit the
stated number of sts through the "purl
bumps" on the back of the chain. To
remove scrap chain, when instructed,
pull out the tail from the last crochet st.

Gently and slowly pull on the tail to unravel the crochet sts, carefully placing
each released knit st on a needle.

3-Needle Bind-Off
1) Hold right sides of pieces together on
2 needles. Insert 3rd needle knitwise into
first st of each needle and wrap yarn
knitwise.
2) Knit these 2 sts together and slip

them off the needles. *Knit the next 2
sts together in the same manner.
3) Slip first st on 3rd needle over 2nd st
and off needle. Rep from * in step 2
across row until all sts are bound off.

Cowl
Cast on 30 sts using provisional cast-on
method. Knit 4 rows.
Next row (RS) K10, turn, place rem 20
sts on st holder.
Working on first 10 sts only, cont in St st
(k on RS, p on WS) until piece measures
approx 26"/66cm. Place sts on st holder.
Place center 10 sts from first holder on
needles, join yarn and work in St st until
piece measures same as first piece. Place
sts on st holder. Repeat for rem 10 sts.

Lightly steam block each length.

Loosely braid the three knitted lengths,
then place all 30 sts on needle once
more. Join yarn and knit 4 rows. Carefully
remove sts from provisional cast-on and
place on needle. Join ends using 3-needle
bind-off; break yarn, leaving long tail.
Allowing outer strips to fold and mini-
mize join, use tail to tack outer strips
over middle strip. ■

Gauge
18 sts and 20 rows to 4"/10cm over St st using size 8 (5mm) needles.
Take time to check gauge.

56

Pretty & Plaited

Triple the style and the warmth by braiding together three loops knit in different stitch and color patterns.

DESIGNED BY INGE SPUNGEN

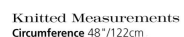

Knitted Measurements
Circumference 48"/122cm
Length 11½"/29cm

Materials
▪ 5 3½oz/100g hanks (each approx 164yd/150m) of Cascade Yarns *Cloud* (merino wool/baby alpaca) in #2121 cadet blue (A) (4)
▪ 1 3½oz/100g hank (each approx 164yd/150m) of Cascade Yarns *Eco Cloud* in #1801 cream (B) (4)
▪ One set (5) size 10½ (6.5mm) double-pointed needles (dpns) *or size to obtain gauge*
▪ Stitch marker and stitch holders

Note
Cowl is made up of 3 tubes, each worked in the round. When the tubes are complete, they are braided together and then the ends of each one are sewn tog to form cowl.

Cowl
TUBE 1
With A, cast on 40 sts. Join, being careful not to twist sts, and place marker (pm) for beg of rnd.

Work in checkerboard pat as foll:
Rnds 1–8 [K5, p5] 4 times around.
Rnds 9–16 [P5, k5] 4 times around.
Rep rnds 1–16 until piece measures approx 38"/96.5cm from beg. Place sts on a st holder.

TUBE 2
Note Tube is worked in a diagonal rib pat, worked in a continuous spiral; the pat will move diagonally by 1 st each rnd. Do *not* begin each rnd with k5, but continue where you left off.
With A, cast on 39 sts. Join, being careful not to twist sts, and work in a continuous rnd, as foll: *K5, p5; rep from * until piece measures same as tube 1. Place sts on a st holder.

TUBE 3
Note Tube is worked by carrying the strand not used *tightly* across the WS of the work to cause a fluted effect.
With A, cast on 42 sts. Join, being careful not to twist sts, and pm for beg of rnd.
Rnds 1–3 *K3 A, k3 B; rep from * around.
Rnds 4–6 *K3 B, k3 A; rep from * around.
Rep rnds 1–6 until piece measures same as tube 1. Place sts on a st holder.

Finishing
Block each tube gently if necessary. Braid the 3 tubes together. Sew the open sts of each tube to its corresponding cast-on edge to form cowl. ▪

Gauge
16 sts and 20 rnds to 4"/10cm over St st using size 10½ (6.5mm) needles.
Take time to check gauge.

57

Honeycomb Heaven

Wear this honeycomb-cabled neckwarmer with the rolled edge
at the top to prettily frame the face.

DESIGNED BY LARS RAINS

Knitted Measurements
Circumference 26"/66cm
Length (with edge unrolled)
6½"/16.5cm

Materials
▓ 1 3½oz/100g hank (each approx
197yd/180m) of Cascade Yarns *Eco Duo*
(baby alpaca/merino wool) in #1706
koala (4)
▓ Size 8 (5mm) circular needle,
24"/60cm long, *or size to obtain gauge*
▓ Cable needle (cn)
▓ Stitch markers

Stitch Glossary
2-st RC Sl 1 st to cn, hold to *back*, k1,
k1 from cn.
2-st LC Sl 1 st to cn, hold to *front*, k1,
k1 from cn.

Honeycomb Cable Pattern
(multiple of 12 sts)
Rnd 1 *K4, 2-st RC, 2-st LC, k4; rep
from * around.
Rnd 2 and all even-numbered rnds
Knit.
Rnd 3 *K2, [2-st RC, 2-st LC] twice, k2;
rep from * around.

Rnd 5 *[2-st RC, 2-st LC] 3 times; rep
from * around.
Rnd 7 *[2-st LC, 2-st RC] 3 times; rep
from * around.
Rnd 9 *K2, [2-st LC, 2-st RC] twice, k2;
rep from * around.
Rnd 11 *K4, 2-st LC, 2-st RC, k4; rep
from * around.
Rnd 12 Knit.
Rep rnds 1–12 for honeycomb cable pat.

Cowl
Cast on 120 sts. Join, taking care not
to twist sts, and place marker for beg
of rnd.
Knit 12 rnds.
Work rnds 1–12 of honeycomb cable pat
twice.
Knit 1 rnd.
Next rnd *K2, p2; rep from * around.
Rep last rnd for k2, p2 rib for 5 rnds
more.
Bind off loosely in rib.▓

Gauge
18 sts and 24 rnds to 4"/10cm over St st using size 8 (5mm) needles.
Take time to check gauge.

Slouchy Stripes

A cooly casual cowl gets a sporty look
from diagonal stripes and a dash of slouch.

DESIGNED BY BONNIE FRANZ

Knitted Measurements
Circumference 30"/76cm
Length 8½"/21.5cm

Materials
▨ 1 3½oz/100g hank (each approx
164yd/150m) of Cascade Yarns *Eco
Cloud* (merino wool/baby alpaca) in
#1809 dove gray (A) (▣4)
▨ 1 3½oz/100g hank (each approx
164yd/150m) of Cascade Yarns *Cloud*
(merino wool/baby alpaca)in #2109
ruby (B)
▨ Size 10½ (6.5mm) circular needle,
24"/60cm long, *or size to obtain gauge*
▨ Stitch marker

Note
Pattern stitch can be worked using chart
or text. Chart is worked in St st (k every
rnd).

COLOR KEY
▨ Dove Gray (A)
■ Ruby (B)

Pattern Stitch
(multiple of 6 sts)
Rnd 1 *K3 B, k3 A; rep from * around.
Rnd 2 *K1 A, k3 B, k2 A; rep from *
around.
Rnd 3 *K2 A, k3 B, k1 A; rep from *
around.
Rnd 4 *K3 A, k3 B; rep from * around.
Rnd 5 *K1 B, k3 A, k2 B; rep from *
around.
Rnd 6 *K2 B, k3 A, k1 B; rep from *
around.
Rep rnds 1–6 for pattern stitch.

Cowl
With A, cast on 126 sts. Join, taking care
not to twist sts, and place marker for
beg of rnd. [Knit 1 rnd, purl 1 rnd] 3
times.
Work in pattern stitch, following text or
chart, until piece measures 7½"/19cm
from beg.
With B, [knit 1 rnd, purl 1 rnd] 3 times.
Bind off.■

Gauge
17 sts and 18 rnds to 4"/10cm over pat stitch using size 10½ (6.5mm) needles.
Take time to check gauge.

59 Traveling Eyelets

Paired eyelets and decreases form a unique motif, finished with seed stitch borders and a button closure.

DESIGNED BY PATTI PIERCE STONE

Knitted Measurements
Circumference (buttoned) 24"/61cm
Length 7"/18cm

Materials
- 1 3½oz/100g hank (each approx 164yd/150m) of Cascade Yarns *Eco Cloud* (merino wool/baby alpaca) in #1803 fawn (4)
- One pair size 8 (5mm) needles *or size to obtain gauge*
- Size F/5 (3.75mm) crochet hook
- Five 1"/2.5cm buttons
- Stitch markers

Cowl
Cast on 38 sts.
Border row 1 (WS) K2, *k1, p1; rep from * to last 2 sts, sl 2 wyif.
Border row 2 (RS) K2, *p1, k1; rep from * to last 2 sts, sl 2 wyif.
Rep border rows 1 and 2 twice more.
Set-up row (WS) K3, p1, k2, [p5, k2] 3 times, p5, [k1, p1] twice, sl 2 wyif.

BEG PATTERN STITCH
Row 1 (RS) K2, p1, k1, p2, [yo, ssk, k3, p2] 3 times, yo, ssk, k3, [p1, k1] twice, sl 2 wyif.
Rows 2, 4, and 6 K3, p1, k2, [p5, k2] 3 times, p5, [k1, p1] twice, sl 2 wyif.

Row 3 K2, p1, k1, p2, [k1, yo, ssk, k2, p2] 3 times, k1, yo, ssk, k2, [p1, k1] twice, sl 2 wyif.
Row 5 K2, p1, k1, p2, [k2, yo, ssk, k1, p2] 3 times, k2, yo, ssk, k1, [p1, k1] twice, sl 2 wyif.
Row 7 K2, p1, k1, p2, [k3, yo, ssk, p2] 3 times, k3, yo, ssk, [p1, k1] twice, sl 2 wyif.
Row 8 Rep row 2.
Rep rows 1–8 for 17 times more.
Next row (RS) K2, p1, k1, p2, [k5, p2] 3 times, k5, [p1, k1] twice, sl 2 wyif.

Work border rows 1 and 2 three times. Bind off purlwise on WS, purling first 2 and last 2 sts tog.
Do *not* fasten off last st, place on crochet hook and work as foll:
Buttonhole edging row Sl st in next 2 sts, [ch 4, skip 4 sts, sl st in each of next 3 sts] 4 times, ch 4, skip 4 sts, sl st in last 2 sts. Fasten off.
Sew buttons approx 4 rows from cast-on edge, opposite buttonholes. ■

Gauge
19 sts and 26 rows to 4"/10cm over pattern st using size 8 (5mm) needles.
Take time to check gauge.

60 Slipping Around

An easy allover slipped-stitch pattern gives a long, loopy cowl extra thickness and texture.

DESIGNED BY AMANDA BLAIR BROWN

Knitted Measurements
Circumference 78"/198cm
Length 7½"/19cm

Materials
- 2 3½oz/100g hanks (each approx 164yd/150m) of Cascade Yarns *Cloud* (merino wool/baby alpaca) each in #2120 true blue (A) and #2100 spring green (B)
- Size 9 (5.5mm) circular needle, 40"/100cm long, *or size to obtain gauge*
- Stitch marker

Cowl
With A, cast on 360 sts. Join, taking care not to twist sts, and place marker for beg of rnd. [Purl 1 rnd, knit 1 rnd] twice, purl 1 rnd.

Note
Either side of the slip stitch fabric looks good. The cowl is shown with the pattern worked from the wrong side.

BEG SLIP STITCH PAT
Rnd 1 (WS) With B, *k1, sl 1 purlwise wyif; rep from * around.
Rnd 2 With B, knit.
Rnd 3 With A, *sl 1 purlwise wyif, k1; rep from * around.
Rnd 4 With A, knit.
Rep rnds 1–4 until piece measures approx 6¾"/17cm from beg, end with a rnd 4.
With A, [purl 1 rnd, knit 1 rnd] twice, purl 1 rnd. Bind off loosely. ■

Gauge
18 sts and 32 rnds to 4"/10cm over St st using size 9 (5.5mm) needle.
Take time to check gauge.

index

A
aran
> Cabled Cowlcho 36

B
Bands of Bold 104
Bobble Flowers 75
bobbles
> Bobble Flowers 75
> Bold Shoulders 82
> Bounty of Bobbles 88
> Cable & Bobble Combo 22
Bold Shoulders 82
Bounty of Bobbles 88
Braided Beauty 142
Budding Out 128
Buttoned Up 108
buttons
> Buttoned Up 108
> Slip-Stitch Style 46
> Traveling Eyelets 150

C
Cable & Bobble Combo 22
Cabled Cowlcho 36
cables
> Bobble Flowers 76
> Budding Out 128
> Buttoned Up 108
> Cable & Bobble Combo 22
> Cabled Cowlcho 36
> Cables on the Edge 123

Curled up in Cables 111
Faux Cables 140
Fishtail Cables 136
High Style 34
Horseshoe Cables 126
Lattice Bliss 84
Ribs with a Twist 78
Travel Time 72
Windswept Cables 102
Cables on the Edge 123
Check Mate 66
chevron
> Chevron Chic 62
> Zigzag Ridges 114
> Chevron Chic 62
colorwork
> Bands of Bold 104
> Check Mate 66
> Full Circle 32
> Granny Square Glam 90
> Intarsia Ribs 56
> Mosaic Diamonds 48
> Pixelation 130
> Pretty & Plaited 144
> Slipping Around 152
> Slip Stitch Stripes 60
> Slouchy Stripes 148
> Snug in Stripes 98
> Stepped-Up Stripes 134
> Sunny Slip Stitch 44
Cozy Quilted 118
crochet

Granny Square Glam 90
Traveling Eyelets 150
Curled Up in Cables 111

D
dropped stitches
> Bold Shoulders 82
> Curled up in Cables 111
> Ribbon Waves 93

E
Entrelac Blocks 39

F
Faux Cables 140
Fetching Feather & Fan 28
Fishtail Cables 136
Frosted Flowers 106
Full Circle 32

G
Gather 'Round 116
geometric
> Intarsia Ribs 56
> Mosaic Diamonds 48
> Stepped-Up Stripes 134
> Zigzag Ridges 114
Gorgeous Gathers 25
Granny Square Glam 90

H
High Style 34

Honeycomb Heaven 146
Horseshoe Cables 126

I
In the Loop 86
Intarsia Ribs 56
It's a Draw 120

L
lace
        Fetching Feather & Fan 28
        Frosted Flowers 106
        Textured Lace 42
        Waves of Lace 100
Lattice Bliss 84
Leaning Tower 20

M
Mosaic Diamonds 48

O
Openwork Flair 50

P
Pixelation 130
Pretty & Plaited 144

R
reversible
        Slipping Around 152
        Snug in Stripes 98
        Wrap Party 53

ribbing
        Bold Shoulders 82
        Buttoned Up 108
        Cable & Bobble Combo 22
        Cables on the Edge 123
        Cozy Quilted 118
        Faux Cables 140
        Fishtail Cables 136
        Granny Square Glam 90
        Honeycomb Heaven 146
        Intarsia Ribs 56
        Openwork Flair 50
        Ribs with a Twist 78
        Riches of Ribs 18
        Snug in Stripes 98
        Waves of Lace 100
        Windswept cables 102
Ribbon Waves 93
Ribs with a Twist 78
Riches of Ribs 18
Ruffled Heathers 80

S
Sea of Scallops 64
Slip Stitch Stripes 60
Slipping Around 152
slip stitch
        Slip Stitch Stripes 60
        Slip-Stitch Style 46
        Sunny Slip Stitch 44
Slip-Stitch Style 46
Slouchy Stripes 148

Snug in Stripes 98
Stepped-Up Stripes 134
Sunny Slip Stitch 44
Sweet & Simple 70

T
Textured Lace 42
Tied in Knots 68
ties
        Bobble Flowers 75
Tiny Bubbles 30
Touch of Texture 96
Travel Time 72
Traveling Eyelets 150

W
Waves of Lace 100
Windswept Cables 102
Woven with Care 132
Wrap Party 53

Z
Zigzag Ridges 114
Zip It Up 138

Things to Know

Abbreviations

approx	approximately		rem	remain(s)(ing)
beg	begin(ning)		rep	repeat
CC	contrasting color		RH	right-hand
ch	chain		rnd(s)	round(s)
cm	centimeter(s)		RS	right side(s)
cn	cable needle		S2KP	slip 2 sts together, knit 1, pass 2 slip stitches over knit 1
cont	continu(e)(ing)			
dc	double crochet		sc	single crochet
dec	decreas(e)(ing)		SKP	slip 1, knit 1, pass slip stitch over
dpn(s)	double-pointed needle(s)			
foll	follow(s)(ing)		SK2P	slip 1, knit 2 together, pass slip stitch over the knit 2 together
g	gram(s)			
inc	increas(e)(ing)			
k	knit		sl	slip
kfb	knit into the front and back of a stitch—one stitch is increased		sl st	slip stitch
			ssk (ssp)	slip next 2 stitches knitwise (purlwise), one at a time; knit (purl) these 2 stitches tog
k2tog	knit 2 stitches together			
LH	left-hand		sssk	slip next 3 stitches knitwise, one at a time; knit these 3 stitches together
lp(s)	loop(s)			
m	meter(s)			
M1	make 1 (knit st) by inserting tip of LH needle from front to back under the strand between the last stitch and the next stitch; knit into the back loop		st(s)	stitch(es)
			St st	stockinette stitch
			tbl	through back loop(s)
			tog	together
			tr	treble crochet
			WS	wrong side(s)
M1 p-st	make 1 purl stitch		wyib	with yarn in back
MC	main color		wyif	with yarn in front
mm	millimeter(s)		yd	yard(s)
oz	ounce(s)		yo	yarn over needle
p	purl		*	repeat directions following * as many times as indicated
p2tog	purl 2 stitches together			
pat(s)	pattern(s)		[ ]	repeat directions inside brackets as many times as indicated
pm	place marker			
psso	pass slip stitch(es) over			

Skill Levels

◼◻◻◻

Ideal first project.

◼◼◻◻

Basic stitches, minimal shaping and simple finishing.

◼◼◼◻

For knitters with some experience. More intricate stitches, shaping, and finishing.

◼◼◼◼

For knitters able to work patterns with complicated shaping and finishing.

Knitting Needles

U.S.	Metric
0	2mm
1	2.25mm
2	2.75mm
3	3.25mm
4	3.5mm
5	3.75mm
6	4mm
7	4.5mm
8	5mm
9	5.5mm
10	6mm
10½	6.5mm
11	8mm
13	9mm
15	10mm
17	12.75mm
19	15mm
35	19mm

Checking Your Gauge

Make a test swatch at least 4"/10cm square. If the number of stitches and rows does not correspond to the gauge given, you must change the needle size. An easy rule to follow is: To get fewer stitches to the inch/cm, use a larger needle; to get more stitches to the inch/cm, use a smaller needle. Continue to try different needle sizes until you get the same number of stitches and rows in the gauge.